# Marek

# German Air Projects
# 1935 - 1945
# vol.3

## Bombers

*Meren-Re*

STRATUS

Published in Poland in 2007
by STRATUS s.c.
Po. Box 123,
27-600 Sandomierz 1, Poland
e-mail:office@mmpbooks.biz
for
Mushroom Model Publications,
36 Ver Road, Redbourn,
AL3 7PE, UK.
e-mail: rogerw@mmpbooks.biz
© 2007 Mushroom Model
Publications.
http://www.mmpbooks.biz

**ISBN**
**978-83-89450-30-2**

*Editor in chief*
**Roger Wallsgrove**

*Editorial Team*
**Bartłomiej Belcarz**
**Robert Pęczkowski**
**Artur Juszczak**
**James Kightly**

*Translation*
**Wojtek Matusiak**

*Scale Plans*
**Marek Ryś**

*DTP*
**Artur Bukowski**

*Printed by:*
*Drukarnia Diecezjalna,*
*ul. Żeromskiego 4,*
*27-600 Sandomierz*
*tel. +48 (15) 832 31 92;*
*fax +48 (15) 832 77 87*
*www.wds.pl marketing@wds.pl*

**PRINTED IN POLAND**

# Contents

# Acknowledgements

The author would like to thank the following people who contributed to the book: Ann Crayfish, Ronnie Olsthoorn, David Myhra, Dan Johnson, and Dieter Herwig.

# The Author

Marek Ryś is an aviation publicist. He is the author of over a dozen books, hundreds of articles, and almost a thousand technical drawings, as well as hundreds of colour 3D images. He works with a select group of publishing houses and magazines in Poland, Europe and the USA. Apart from aviation history he is interested in history and theory of art and film, in music (especially progressive metal and rock), and in playing on the guitar, in digital 3D technology. He is a great fan of open source software (he uses Blender, Pov Ray, Gimp, and Inkscape). You can visit his website at: www.airart3d.xt.pl

# Note on dimensions

In certain cases the dimensions of the aircraft's three-view drawings differ from some official technical data. This is not an error, as all the drawings were based on original German sources - drawings and data sheets, but of course there were variations in even official sources. The subject aircraft were concepts, rather than actual physical objects, and many went through many different concept stages, which can easily result in apparently conflicting information, so the drawings should be regarded as illustrative only.

# ARADO

## Ar 234 — bomber versions

The Arado Ar 234 "Blitz" was the second jet aircraft manufactured for the Luftwaffe. Designed and built as a bomber and reconnaissance aircraft, it was used in substantial numbers during the war. Many fighter variant projects were also prepared.

The principal production version was the twin-engined Ar 234B-1/B-2. However, by the end of the war some 19 examples (mainly prototypes) of the Ar 234C variant were built, this being a four-engined version, powered by less powerful BMW 003 engines. The layout and equipment of the cockpit were completely redesigned and the engines were located under the wings in two double 'siamesed' nacelles. Otherwise, the variant was very little changed from the B version. It was an all-metal high-wing monoplane with an enclosed cockpit and tricycle undercarriage that retracted into the fuselage.

Because the new cockpit was accepted as standard for further development of the aircraft, subsequent versions were based on the Ar 234C-3 layout. Initially, they differed little from their predecessor. The Ar 234 C-4 was a reconnaissance C-3, with reduced armament. The Ar 234C-5 was much more interesting; a two-seater bomber with another variant of the cockpit. The two-seater cockpits were to be built in two variants: 'clean', or with a tear-drop fairing over the navigator's head, the so-called *sichtbeule*. The latter variant was intended for the night fighter version.

In the 'clean' cockpit, the pilot and bomb-aimer were seated side-by-side, although the pilot's seat was a little higher. Ar 234V32 and V33 were intended to be the production pattern aircraft for the C-5. The V34 was going to be powered by two Heinkel HeS 011A engines, which would probably have given it better performance. Difficult wartime conditions, however, and problems with deliveries as well as delays of the HeS 011 programme resulted in the development of the 'low cost' version, the Ar 234C-8, which was fitted with two

Jumo 004D engines and the top speed was expected to drop by 90 km/h.

Apart from modifying the aircraft itself, work also continued on the armament it would carry. One of the most advanced projects was to enable the V34 to carry the 1570 kg Fritz X guided bomb. The large size of the weapon (3.26 m long) made it difficult to attach it under the fuselage. Surviving drawings suggest that it was tried in various positions forward and aft of the machine's centre of gravity. The fuselage had to have a deep cut-out in the area, which in turn entailed changes to the internal equipment of the bomber. There were also plans to attach a BT 1400 torpedo-bomb or Blohm & Voss L11 glide-bomb, and changes to the Hs 293 rocket bomb were also much advanced. A special variant of the bomb was developed for the Ar 234 (Hs 293 V6 was going to be its prototype) with smaller and differently-positioned cruise engines, and with a folding fin. The work started after the Ar 234 S9 and then S10 were used to test a standard Hs 293, but insufficient ground clearance of the attached bomb prevented its use in practice.

C series variants offered essentially just cosmetic changes in the airframe. In June of 1944, the RLM showed interest in suggestions, expressed some time before by the designers of the Blitz, to fit the aircraft with swept wings.

The previously-used straight wings worked well at speeds of up to 801 km/h (498 mph), but at any greater speed, their characteristics deteriorated significantly. As early as 1942 Lehmann obtained a patent (no. 844723) for a wing with variable sweep along the leading edge, combined with the relative thickness decreasing along the span. This allowed maintainance of the same flow characteristics along the entire wing at high critical Mach number. Because of the scope and demands of the work developing the principal versions of the Blitz, Kosin and Lehmann were prevented from initiating detailed work on such a swept wing. However, they did make calculations and planned engineering solutions on their own initiative. Eventually, on 3 June 1944, they showed the drawings of proposed high speed wing variants to Knemeyer*, and they were officially commissioned to start detailed analysis of the problem.

As a result of the work they produced five different wings. The first project was the Versuchsflügel I. Its leading edge sweep was 33.5° at the root, 23° in the centre, and 19.5° at the tips. Wing span was going to be 13.20 m. Soon afterwards this was discarded for the Versuchsflügel II, with a sweep angle of 37° at the root and 23° at the wing tips. The Versuchsflügel III was a conventional wing planform but with laminar-flow wing. The Versuchsflügel IV combined the features of the second and third projects. The last project was the Versuchsflügel V, with a straight leading edge swept at 35°. The latter variant was built as a model for comparative trials during wind-tunnel testing at the DVL (Deutsche Versuchsanstalt für Luftfahrt — German Aviation Test Centre).

All of the proposed wings were going to have all-metal construction, but because they needed to start their flight testing as quickly as possible, it was considered expedient to replace metal with wood, and also this concept existed for the Ar 234B and Ar 234C wings. Kosin himself was sceptical about the wooden wing, assuming that the material was not suited for very high speed aircraft.

In mid-1944 it was decided that four Ar 234 prototypes would be used for tests: V16 (PH+SX, W.Nr. 130026), V18 (W.Nr. 130028), V26 (W.Nr. 130066) and V30. The first of these was to be fitted with two BMW 003R composite engines, made up of the 7.85 kN thrust BMW 003A jet and the

9.81 kN BMW 718 rocket booster. The remaining machines would be powered by four BMW 003A-1s. On 5 November 1944, during a meeting with Knemeyer, tests of new wings on the Ar 234 were discussed, and advantages of using results obtained in previously-completed practical tests were stressed. At this point, the number of experimental machines allocated to the Versuchsflügel programme were increased. A document of January 16, 1945 analysed once more the allocation of existing and planned prototypes (V18 to V40), changing the assignments of some of these and suspending some secondary trial programmes. Existing machines were going to be converted by the so-called 'Development workshops' (Entwicklung Betrieb I; EB I in short) at Brandenburg.

As a result of the reorganisation, the new wing tests were going to involve:

- Ar 234 V16 — fitted with two BMW 003R engines and the Versuchsflügel II wing;
- Ar 234 V18 — fitted with four BMW 003A engines and the Versuchsflügel II wing: expected date of completion of the conversion — 10 March 1945;
- Ar 234 V19 — ditto; expected date of delivery to the EB I — 30 March 1945; expected date of completion of the conversion — 5 May 1945;
- Ar 234 V21 — fitted with four BMW 003A engines and the Versuchsflügel IV wing; expected date of delivery to the EB I — 30 April 1945; expected date of completion of the conversion — 31 May 1945;
- Ar 234 V29 — fitted with four BMW 003A engines and the Versuchsflügel III wing; expected date of delivery to the EB I — 15 February 1945; expected date of completion of the conversion — 31 March 1945;
- Ar 234 V35 — two-seater, fitted with two HeS 011 engines and the Versuchsflügel III wing;

---

* Siegfried Knemeyer, the former head of the German RLM ( The Reichsluftfahrtministerium), the Third Reich's Air Ministry for aircraft development for the Luftwaffe

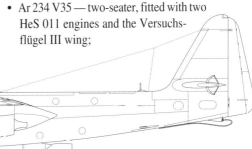

*Ar 234C-5 with BT 1400 bomb*
© *Marek Ryś 2007*

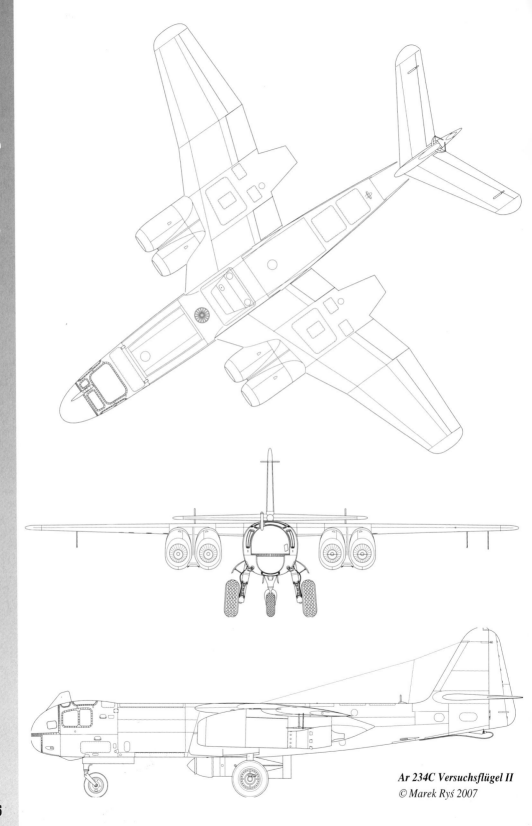

*Ar 234C Versuchsflügel II*
© Marek Ryś 2007

*Ar 234C-3*
© Marek Ryś 2007

- Ar 234 V36 — fitted with two HeS 011 engines and the Versuchsflügel II wing;
- Ar 234 V37 — fitted with two HeS 011 engines and the Versuchsflügel IV wing;
- Ar 234 V38 — fitted with two HeS 011 engines and the Versuchsflügel IIIa wing (with rounded leading edge and without flaps);
- Ar 234 V39 — ditto;
- Ar 234 V40 — ditto.

The plan was that along with the test wings, a modified, swept, horizontal tail would also be fitted.

Very little was accomplished of these ambitious plans, and most prototypes were never built at all. The completed V18, V19 and V21 were eventually left in the original configuration (with a standard wing), as the end of the war prevented their conversion. The only aircraft to reach a more advanced stage was the Ar 234 V16, built at Düsseldorf. At the war's end new wings were undergoing assembly onto the fuselage. The work was terminated when British troops captured the factory in April 1945. Not realising the value of their find, the soldiers who entered the plant destroyed the aircraft before it was inspected by experts.

Another bomber project based on the Ar 234 was the Ar 234D-2, powered by two HeS 011A engines. The aircraft featured another cockpit

design and its length extended to 12.78 m. Bombs of up to 1,000 kg could be carried both under the fuselage and under the wings, but not all 3 in the same time.

Due to its peculiar design (i.e. the absence of a bomb bay), the Ar 234 could not become a typical bomber. Different versions were, however, considered as potential carrier aircraft in the Mistel system.

Specifications:

| Version: | Ar 234C-5 | Ar 234 D-2 |
|---|---|---|
| wing span | 14.41m (47.27ft) | 14.41m (47.27ft) |
| length | 12.90m (42.32ft) | 12.78m (41.92ft) |
| height | 4.28m (14.04ft) | 4.28m (14.04ft) |
| wing area | 27.0 m$^2$ (290.63 sq ft) | 27.0m$^2$ (290.63 sq ft) |
| empty weight | 6,570 kg (14,484.38 lb) | 5,450 kg (12,015.20 lb) |
| take-off weight | 11,150 kg (24,581.56 lb) | 9,850 kg (21,715.55 lb) |
| top speed | 870 km/h (541 mph) | 795 km/h (494 mph) |
| range | 1,020 km (634 miles) | 1,420 km (882 miles) |

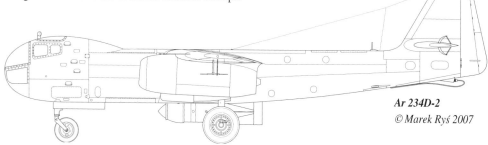

*Ar 234D-2*
© Marek Ryś 2007

# PTL-STRÄHLBOMBER

One of the new engine types that appeared in concept form in Germany during the war was the turbo-prop engine: it combined the advantages of a propeller with those of a jet. Several such power-plants were developed, including the Daimler Benz DB 021, the BMW 028, and the Jumo 022.

During the summer of 1943, Arado prepared a preliminary project for a turbo-prop bomber,

known in documents as the PTL-Strählbomber. The power plant would consist of two BMW 028 or DB 021 engines, rated at some 6,200 hp, located in nacelles over the wings. This layout was selected in order to maintain its shape as a compact low-wing monoplane. The forward fuselage housed the cockpit for a crew of two or three. Fuel tanks and equipment bays were located further aft and conventional tail surfaces were mounted on the rear fuselage. Wings were swept, and housed further fuel tanks and the main wheel wells. The nose wheel unit retracted into the fuselage. Take-off weight of the aircraft could reach 33,700 kg, and the take-off run was estimated at a short 580 m (1,900 ft).

Turbo-prop propulsion was also considered for the Ar 234, but this did not proceed beyond project status.

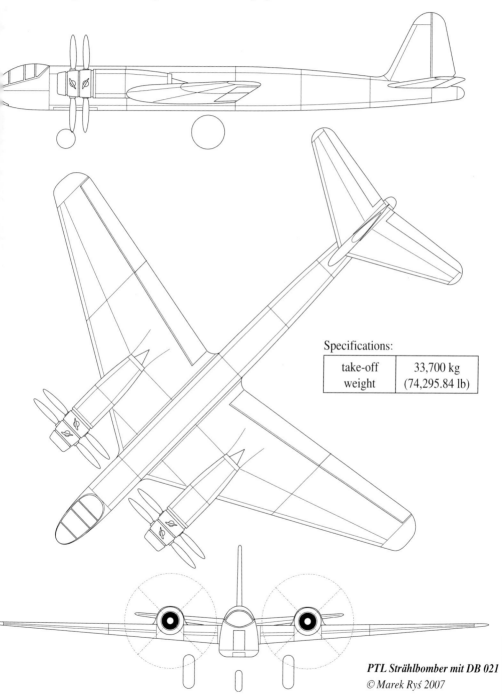

Specifications:

| take-off weight | 33,700 kg (74,295.84 lb) |
|---|---|

*PTL Strählbomber mit DB 021*
© *Marek Ryś 2007*

# E.395

As part of the Ar 234 development work, in 1944 its designers preparedan enlarged variant, called E.395.01, powered by four HeS 011A jet engines located in twinned nacelles. The design was largely based on the Ar 234D, but the cockpit was extensively modified, with reduced glazing surface. The aircraft was 16.85 m long: stretched by almost 3m.

The wing was completely new. It was swept with a varying sweep angle along the leading edge. The wing was going to have extensive high-lift devices consisting of flaps and slats, in addition to ailerons. Oddly, the horizontal tail was left unchanged. The undercarriage also did not differ much from that of the 'classic' Blitz. Because of the small cross-section of the fuselage, bombs had to be carried under the fuselage on external racks. Defensive armament was going to consist of two forward-firing 20mm MG 151/20 cannon, two similar cannon firing backwards, and one downward-firing 13mm MG 131 machine gun. The downward-firing cannon and the cannon mounted in the rear fuselage were aimed via a periscopic sight. Normal bomb load was 1,500 kg, and with reduced fuel tankage, it could even go up to 3,000kg.

Apart from the project with the swept wing, there was also a version with a straight wing and a span increased from 15.5m to 17.6m -- it seems that this layout was the ultimate variant or the aircraft

For completeness, it is worth mentioning the E.395.02, which was more of a fighter-bomber (or Zerstörer (destroyer)) than a classic bomber. The aircraft was similar in size to the Ar 234: essentially only the cockpit was changed, to include a classic canopy. The power plant would consist of two HeS 011A engines.

| Specifications | E.395.01: |
|---|---|
| wing span | 17.60 m (57.74 ft) |
| length | 16.85 m (55.28 ft) |
| height | 5.30 m (17.38 ft) |
| wing area | 40.00 m² (430.57 sq ft) |
| empty weight | 9,450 kg (20,833.70 lb) |
| take-off weight | 15,800 kg (34,833.06 lb) |
| top speed | 887 km/h (551 mph) at an altitude of 6,000 m (19,700 ft) |
| ceiling | 14,500 m (47,600 ft) |
| range | 1,500 km (932 miles) |

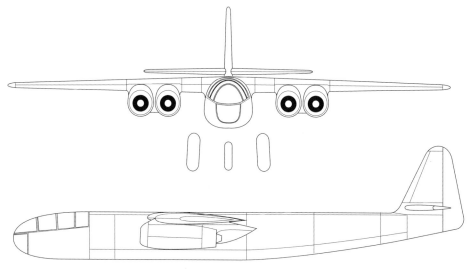

*E.395.1 version with straight wing*
*© Marek Ryś 2007*

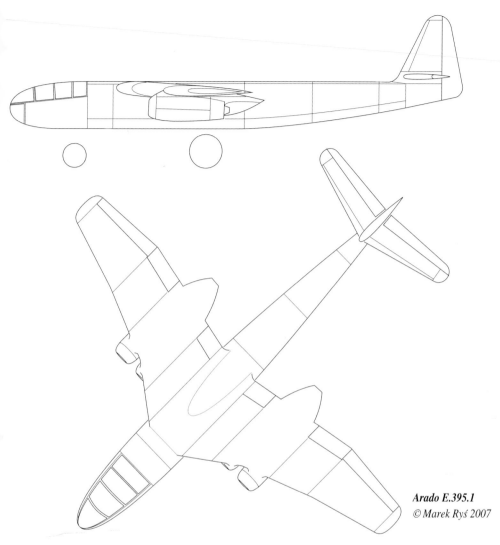

*Arado E.395.1*
© *Marek Ryś 2007*

# E.340

The Luftwaffe's principal bombers, apart from the He 111, were the Ju 88 and the Do 217. However, for the duration of the war, the Luftwaffe failed to find successors for these aircraft. Although the Ju 88 remained effective, the Do 217 was becoming rapidly obsolete. Already, at the beginning of July 1939, the RLM issued the 'Bomber-B' specification. This was going to be a twin-engined aircraft that was able to carry 4,800 kg of bombs and to reach the British Isles. It was a requirement that the machine should be capable of dive bombing attacks, and should also be able to reach high altitudes. The power plant would consist of Jumo 222 or DB 604 engines. At the time, both of these engine types were in the early stages of development.

One of the companies participating in the competition was Arado, with its E.340 project. This was a very unusual aircraft, with a twin-boom layout, central fuselage nacelle, and engines located in two 'fuselages' that ended with twin vertical and horizontal tails. The latter was odd in that each 'fuselage' had one tailplane. The straight wing consisted of the rectangular wing centre section, and tapered outer sections. They were fitted with ailerons, flaps and slats, and housed fuel tanks inside.

The fuselage nacelle contained an extensively-glazed cockpit for the crew of three, and a bomb bay. The aircraft would be powered by two Jumo 222 or DB 604 engines driving three-bladed propellers. Defensive armament was located in five remotely controlled positions: two 13mm MG 131 in an FDL 131/7 turret on the fuselage, another two

in a similar turret under the fuselage, one MG 131 in a ball yoke at the rear of the fuselage nacelle and two MG 131s in ball yokes at the ends of the fuselage booms. The aircraft was going to carry 4,800kg of bombs in the bomb bay.

The competitors (Ju 288, Do 317, Fw 191) were much more traditional in their designs, and this was appreciated by the RLM, who rejected the Arado project. Incidentally, this was the only participant in the Bomber-B competition that was not eventually built.

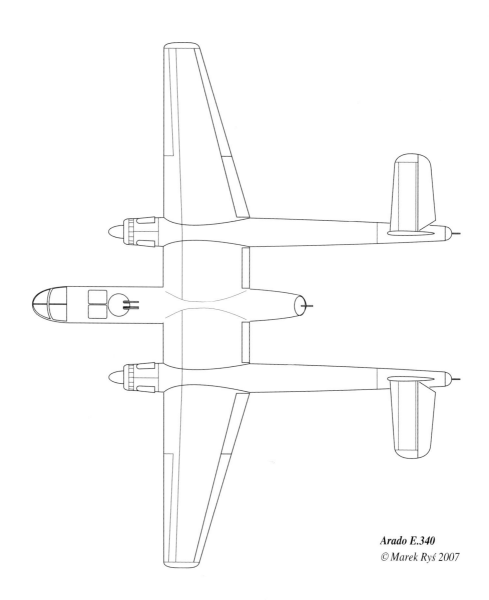

*Arado E.340*
© *Marek Ryś 2007*

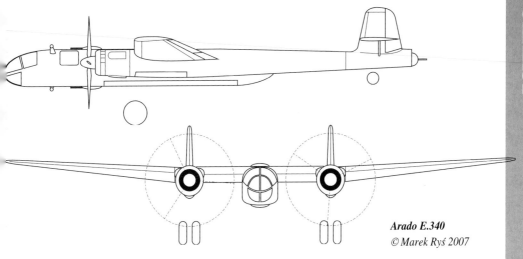

*Arado E.340*
© *Marek Ryś 2007*

| Specifications | E.340: |
|---|---|
| wing span | 23.00 m (75.45 ft) |
| length | 18.65 m (61.18 ft) |
| height | 4.10 m (13.45 ft) |
| wing area | 69.00 m² (742.73 sq ft) |
| take-off weight | 19,300 kg (42,549.25 lb) |
| top speed | 600 km/h (373 mph) at an altitude of 7,000 m (23,000 ft) |
| range | 3,600 km (2,237 miles) |
| endurance | 7 h 20 min. |

# E.470

In 1941 Arado started work on a giant bomber, its range calculated at 15,000 km. This was the project designated E.470. Its design referred both to the similar Focke Wulf project (P 03.10225-20) and to an earlier Arado design, the E.340.

The E.470 was a twin-boom design. The short fuselage was the central element, housing a four-seat cockpit, and attached to the wing centre section. The fuselage booms were an extension of the outer engine nacelles and ended with twin vertical tails connected by a tailplane. The huge wing centre section had rectangular shape in plan view, and its thickness reached a remarkable 2 m, allowing it room to house both the fuel tanks and the bomb bay. Outer wing sections were tapered.

Four E.470 variants were designed:
- Project A — was going to be powered by four 3,500 hp 24-cylinder DB 613 in-line engines (in fact each of these engines was a pair of coupled DB 603s). The wing span was going to reach 47.30m;
- Project B — power plant would consist of six DB 613 engines and the wing span was planned at 54.00m;
- Project C — power plant of four DB 613s and wing span of 60.00m;
- Project D — again six DB 613s and wing span of 58.50m;
- Project E — principal variant fitted with four DB 613s and wing span of 68.50m. It was going to carry a total of 5,000kg of armament, which included, apart from bombs, several remotely-controlled turrets (armed most probably with MG 151 cannon or MG 131 machine guns).

In all the cases, engines were fitted with turbo-superchargers. There was also a project to

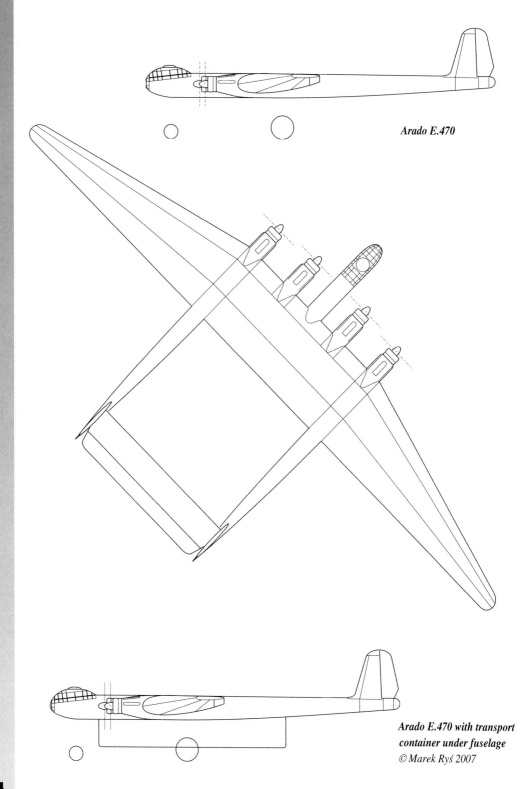

*Arado E.470*

*Arado E.470 with transport
container under fuselage*
© Marek Ryś 2007

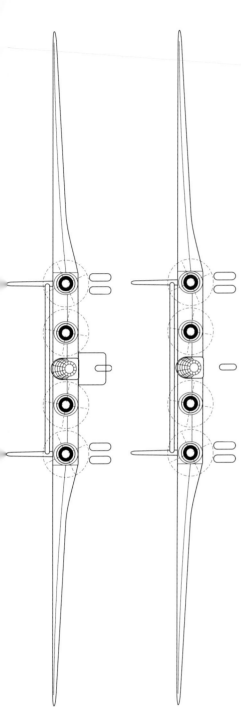

supplement the four DB 613s with two jet engines, on pylons under the wing centre section (project of 19 December 1941).

The E.470F (Project F) variant was going to be a transport aircraft, with the ability to carry 39 tonnes payload. This was going to be carried in a special container attached under the wing centre section. A special attachment was designed, allowing for the container to be fitted and removed within a few minutes.

The undercarriage of the giant was going to consist of twin main wheel units, retracting into the fuselage booms, and a single nose wheel unit retracted into the 'fuselage'.

The RLM rejected the Arado proposal without explanation. Probably the layout was simply too innovative.

| Specifications | E.470E: |
| --- | --- |
| wing span | 68.50 m (224.73 ft) |
| length | 31.00 m(101.70 ft) |
| wing area | 392.00 m² (4,219.59 sq ft) |
| take-off weight | 130,000 kg (286,600 ft) |
| top speed | 530 km/h (330 mph) |
| ceiling | 11,000 m (36,089 ft) |
| range | 14,900 km (9,258 miles) |

# E.555

The E.555 was probably the most technologically advanced Arado bomber project. Work on the E.555 commenced at the end of 1943 in the department at Landeshut (now Kamienna Góra in Poland), and the project was led by Dr. Ing. W. Laute.

From the outset the aircraft featured a very advanced layout (the same layout that was intended for the E.581 fighter), in the form of a flying wing with a vertical tail. Theoretical assumptions were based on a study of the flying wing layout for a long range and high speed aircraft, authored by Kosin and Lehmann. The entire project included 15 variants of the aircraft, some of completely different designs.

On April 20, 1944, the Arado proposal was presented to the RLM. Based on this proposal, shortly thereafter the Ministry issued a specification for a new long range bomber for the Luftwaffe.

*Arado E.470 with transport container under fuselage*

*Arado E.470*
*© Marek Ryś 2007*

The principal criterion was an ability to carry 4,000 kg of bombs over a distance of 5,000 km. For aerodynamic reasons, the flying wing layout was perfectly suited for this kind of performance, as it offered significant useful space for armament and fuel, while being compact and of relatively low weight.

Arado replied to the RLM specification with the E.555/1 project. It was a three-seat, all-metal bomber in the flying wing layout, but with a rather unusual fuselage. This was circular in cross-section; its diameter little more than the airfoil thickness at the wing root, and was blended with the wing. The forward section housed a well glazed cockpit, and the bomb bay was aft of the cockpit.

The wing of the E.555/1 was made up of swept, tapered inner sections, while the outer panels had forward swept trailing edges. In addition, the outer sections were anhedral. Tapered fins were located at the joint of the inner and outer wing sections (6.2m from the centreline). The tricycle undercarriage retracted into the wings and the fuselage, and the aircraft had a total of 10 wheels: two in the nose wheel unit and four each in the main undercarriage. The plan was to use additional take-off wheels, jettisoned after use, because the bomber would have a take-off weight of 24,000 kg. The aircraft was to be powered by six BMW 003A engines located side-by-side on a special pylon above the fuselage. The engine set was split into three twin units. The central unit was located just above the fuselage, while the two side ones were slightly to the rear and placed in a higher position. However, the engine thrust would still have been insufficient, and it was proposed instead that the ultimate variant, the E.555/2, would have four BMW 018s. Two of these would be located above the wing and two below it.

The defensive armament of the E.555/1 was going to consist of two forward-firing 30mm MK 103 cannon in the wing roots; two MG 151/20 cannon in a position immediately aft of the cockpit; and two similar cannon in a remotely-controlled position at the rear of the fuselage.

The E.555/3 project repeated the general concept of the E.555/1, but would be powered by two BMW 018 jet engines. One of these would be located above the fuselage, and the other below it,

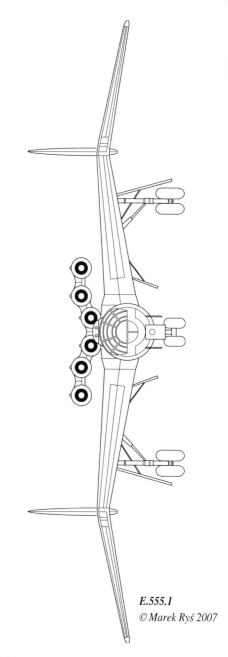

**E.555.1**
*© Marek Ryś 2007*

which necessitated removing the tail gun position. The crew was reduced to two. The main wheel units were going to consist of four wheels each, rather than two.

The E.555/4 was expected to have three BMW 018 engines: two of these under the wing and one above. The aircraft's wing span would be slightly reduced.

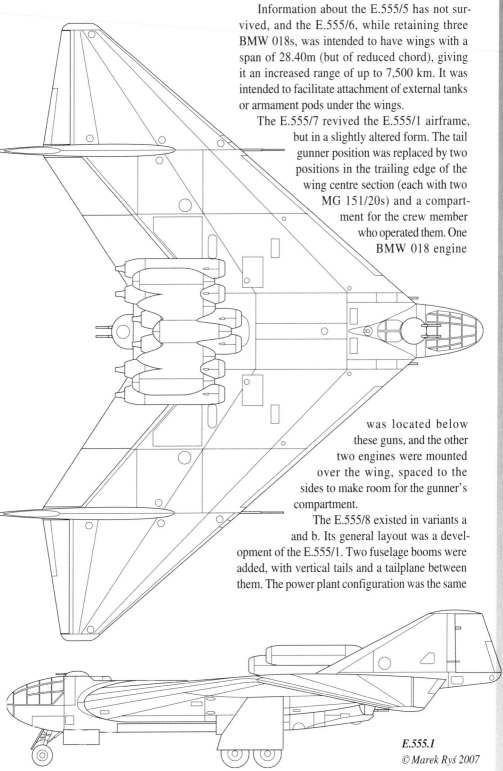

Information about the E.555/5 has not survived, and the E.555/6, while retaining three BMW 018s, was intended to have wings with a span of 28.40m (but of reduced chord), giving it an increased range of up to 7,500 km. It was intended to facilitate attachment of external tanks or armament pods under the wings.

The E.555/7 revived the E.555/1 airframe, but in a slightly altered form. The tail gunner position was replaced by two positions in the trailing edge of the wing centre section (each with two MG 151/20s) and a compartment for the crew member who operated them. One BMW 018 engine

was located below these guns, and the other two engines were mounted over the wing, spaced to the sides to make room for the gunner's compartment.

The E.555/8 existed in variants a and b. Its general layout was a development of the E.555/1. Two fuselage booms were added, with vertical tails and a tailplane between them. The power plant configuration was the same

*E.555.1*
© *Marek Ryś 2007*

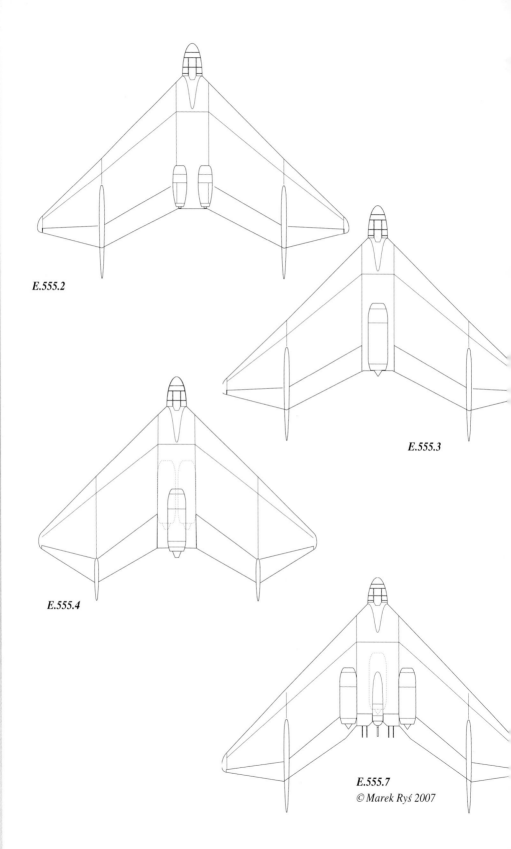

E.555.2

E.555.3

E.555.4

E.555.7
© Marek Ryś 2007

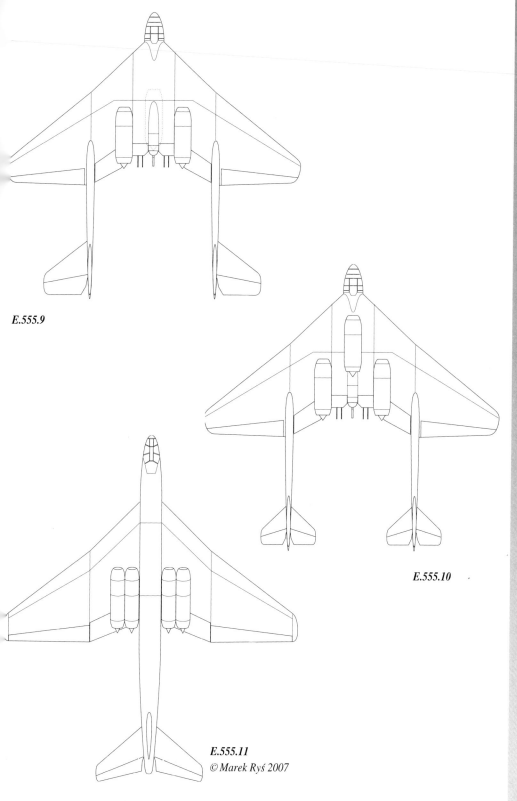

E.555.9

E.555.10

E.555.11
© Marek Ryś 2007

as in the E.555/7, but the rear-firing defensive armament was discarded.

The E.555/9 reintroduced the rear-firing defensive guns, and the tailplane was split in two smaller tailplanes, each fitted on the outer sides of the fins, to give a clear field of fire for the rear-firing cannon.

To counter the reduced efficiency of such a tailplane design, the E.555/10 featured two additional tailplanes on the inboard sides of the fins.

The layout of the E.555/11 was quite different. This was almost a classic bomber with a long fuse-lage and swept tail, and the only feature that linked it with the preceding projects was the wing plan. Four Jumo 012 engines (in pairs) were mounted on the upper surface. It was expected that the aircraft would attain a speed of some 1,020km/h, and no defensive armament was planned.

Work on the E.555/1 (as the principal version) was well advanced, and results of initial calcula-tions were very promising. However, on December 28, 1944, the entire project was cancelled, as the Third Reich desperately needed fighters, not bombers.

| Specifications | | E.555/1 | E.555/3 | E.555/6 | E.555/7 | E.555/10 | E.555/11 |
|---|---|---|---|---|---|---|---|
| Wing span | m | 21.20 | 21.20 | 28.4 | 25.20 | 23.66 | 23.66 |
| | ft | 69.55 | 69.55 | 93.17 | 82.67 | 77.62 | 77.62 |
| Length | m | 18.40 | 18.40 | 18.40 | 18.80 | 19.20 | 25.10 |
| | ft | 60.36 | 60.36 | 60.36 | 61.67 | 62.99 | 82.34 |
| Height | m | 5.00 | 5.00 | 3.74 | 3.65 | N/A | 4.10 |
| | ft | 16.40 | 16.40 | 12.27 | 11.97 | N/A | 13.45 |
| Wing area | m² | 125.00 | 125.00 | 160 | 160 | 140 | 140 |
| | sq ft | 1,345.53 | 1,345.53 | 1,722.28 | 1,722.28 | 1,506.99 | 1,506.99 |
| Max. take-off weight | kg | 24,000 | 25,200 | N/A | 41,300 | 47,845 | 47,000 |
| | lb | 52,911 | 55,557 | N/A | 91,051 | 105,480 | 10,3617 |
| Top speed | km/h | 860 | 875-915 | 875-920 | 950 | 920 | 950-1,020 |
| | mph | 534 | 544- 569 | 544-572 | 590 | 572 | 590-634 |
| Ceiling | m | 13,000-15,000 | N/A | N/A | 14,700 | 14,500 | N/A |
| | ft | 42,651-49,213 | N/A | N/A | 48,228 | 47,572 | N/A |
| Range | km | 4,800 | 4,000 | 5,400-7,500 | 4,500 | 6,400 | 7,000-8,000 |
| | miles | 2,983 | 2,485 | 3,355-4,660 | 2,796 | 3,977 | 4,350-4,971 |

# BLOHM & VOSS

## P.184.01

The design office of Blohm und Voss, headed by Dr. Ing. Richard Vogt, may not have had many spectacular successes in terms of mass-produced aircraft, but each of their designs set new standards in terms of the technological capabilities of the German aircraft industry. From the avant-garde, asymmetric Bv 141 up to the huge Bv 222 flying boat, each 'Bv' aircraft was innovative.

Of course, many of these novelties never proceeded beyond the drawing board. This was the case with the P.184.01 bomber, which combined a very simple aerodynamic concept with a result-ing good performance. The aircraft was going to be a four-engined, low-wing monoplane of all-metal construction. The fuselage, which was of circular cross-section, housed in its nose section an extensively glazed cockpit for the crew of five. Further aft lay the bomb bay (in the reconnaissance variant, photographic equipment or additional fuel tanks could be fitted there) and a fuel tank 1.8m long. A classic tail was fitted on the rear fuselage, immediately forward of the tail gun position.

The wings comprised a rectangular wing centre section and tapered outer sections. Their internal design was very interesting, based on a box-like spar, which also acted as a fuel tank. The skin was

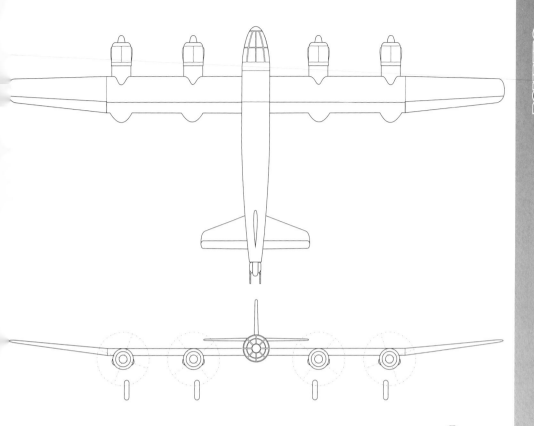

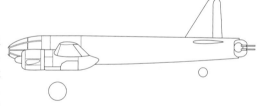

*Blohm und Voss P.184.01*

© *Marek Ryś 2007*

made of steel sheets 2mm thick. The wing was fitted with flaps and ailerons. Although the fashion in various projects was for tricycle undercarriages, Vogt selected a classic tail wheel design for his P.184. There were four individual main wheels, retracting into the engine nacelles. The aircraft would be powered by four 1,950 hp BMW 801E radials, located in nacelles under the wing centre section.

Aiming for a simple design, Vogt introduced (heavier) steel components in place of aluminium ones, the latter metal being in short supply. Generally, the entire P.184 project was aimed at maximum simplicity and low cost of construction.

Armament for the bomber was going to consist of machine guns and cannon located in remotely-controlled dorsal, ventral, and tail turrets. The bomb bay could accommodate up to 4,000 kg of bombs.

The RLM was not enthusiastic about the P.184, as the project offered unspectacular performance in exchange for construction using non-strategic materials.

| Specifications | P.184.01 |
| --- | --- |
| wing span | 35.80 m (117.45 ft) |
| length | 17.30 m (56.75 ft) |
| height | 6.60 m (21.65 ft) |
| wing area | 82.00 m² (882.66 sq ft) |
| take-off weight | 43,225 kg (95,295 lb) |
| top speed | 500 km/h (311mph) |
| ceiling | 8,840 m (29,000 ft) |
| range | 7,500 km (4,660 miles) |

# P.188

The P.188 of 1943 was without a doubt the most advanced bomber designed at Blohm & Voss. Its particular feature was the wing planform in shape of the letter 'W'. Inboard wing sections were swept back (approx. 20°), and the outboard sections swept forward. Additionally, the angle of attack could be changed between 3° and 12° during take-off. This was mainly to compensate for the aerodynamic flexing of the wing tips, which in this layout, were subjected to higher than normal air pressure. Wings housed additional fuel tanks, and their construction was based on duralumin. Flaps were made of wood, as were the rudder and elevator. Four 9.95 kN Jumo 004C jet engines were located in individual nacelles under the inboard wing sections.

The fuselage was made up of three sections. The principal, central section, was designed as a steel shell (the rest of the fuselage was intended to be made of duralumin), housing the 6,800 litre fuel tank and the bomb bay. Location of these two components almost exactly at the aircraft's centre of gravity enhanced its stability in flight. The forward section had a pressurised cockpit for the crew of two and the nose wheel well, and the rear section, with a conventional, but swept, tail, were attached to the centre section. The rear section also housed the tail undercarriage well, as the P.188 featured tandem main wheels. The nose and tail units had twin wheels, and stability was provided by additional small side wheels which retracted into the wings. Because the bomber was designed as a high-wing monoplane, these additional wheels had extremely long legs. An air brake was fitted at the rear of the fuselage, to assist in reducing the landing run.

The aircraft in this configuration was designated the P.188.01. Nothing is known about the defensive armament, but it can reasonably be assumed that it would include remotely-controlled turrets with MG 151 cannon or MG 131 machine guns.

The second version, P.188.02, differed significantly from its predecessor. It had a new cockpit, its canopy protruding beyond the fuselage outline.

This was taken over from the Junkers Ju 488 project without any significant changes. Twin vertical tails were used. Detailed information about the armament survives: the P.188.02 was going to have two forward-firing 20mm MG 151/20 cannon in the fuselage, two similar rearward-firing ones in the fuselage, and two 13mm MG 131 machine guns in the FHL 131Z (FHL - Ferngerichtette Hecklafete)- remotely-controlled turret at the rear of the fuselage. The navigator, who controlled them, had a periscopic sight. The plan was to to fit two more fuselage turrets: dorsal and ventral.

The P.188.03 largely revived the P.188.01 design, although the engines were grouped in pairs in large nacelles under the wings.

The ultimate variant was going to be the P.188.04, which combined features of the P.188.02 (twin fins) and P.188.03 (twin-engine nacelles). Of course the aircraft was going to carry full defensive armament:three turrets with twin MG 131 machine guns and four MG 151/20 cannon.

The fuselage was dramatically slimmed down and its cross-section seriously reduced. Because of this, the bombs needed to be carried under the wings. The RLM failed to approve of the expected performance of the aircraft, and the advanced aerodynamic concept did nothing to make it popular, so the Ministry stopped all work on the bomber.

|  | P.188.01 | P.188.02: |
|---|---|---|
| wing span | 27.00m (88.58ft) | 27.00m (88.58ft) |
| length | 17.60m (57.74ft) | 17.60m (57.74ft) |
| height | 4.10m (13.45ft) | 3.45m (11.31ft) |
| wing area | 60.00m² (645.85 sq ft) | 69.42m² (747.25 sq ft) |
| empty weight | 13,400 kg (29,542 lb) | N/A |
| take-off weight | 26,800kg (59,084 lb) | 24,000kg (52,911 lb) |
| top speed | 860-910 km/h (534-565 mph ) | 820 km/h (510 mph) |
| range | 4,800 km (2,983 miles) | 2,270 km (1,410 miles) |

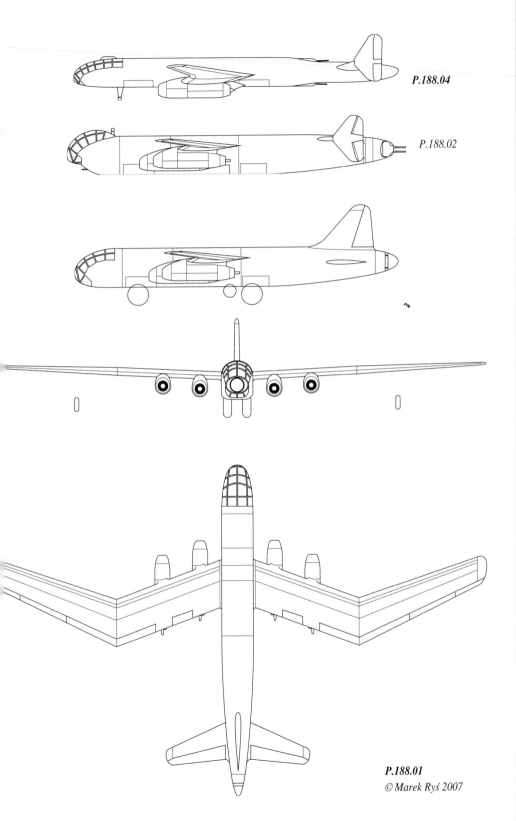

P.188.04

P.188.02

P.188.01
© Marek Ryś 2007

# Bv 250

The prototype of the Bv 238 V1 flying boat, a development of the Bv 222, was first flown on 10 March 1944. This was going to be a long-range patrol and reconnaissance aircraft, but its use was limited to seas or areas with large lakes. In parallel with the basic version, a land-based variant was also under development, initially designated the Bv 238 Land, and then the Bv 250. The Bv 250 was also inspired by a slightly earlier project called the P.161.

According to Vogt's calculations and the assumptions of the design team, the aircraft was going to be able to carry a load of 45,000kg over a distance of 2,500km. In the bomber variant, with a bomb load of 20,000kg, the range was going to reach 7,000km - and with 4,000kg of bombs even as far as 10,000 km. The aircraft would be able to fly even further in its reconnaissance variant, the range extending to 15,000 km.

The Bv 250 inherited the general layout of the Bv 238. It was a six-engined high-wing monoplane of all-metal construction. The entire bottom portion of the fuselage was replaced, as this now housed wells with twelve-wheel bogies (three rows of four wheels) in tandem under the central section, supported additionally by the nose wheel and two stabilising wheels retracting into the wings. The main plane consisted of a rectangular wing centre section and tapered outer sections. The Bv 250 would be powered by six 1,950 hp Daimler Benz DB 603E engines. The heavy defensive armament included MG 151 cannon and MG 131 machine guns located in no less than six turrets on the sides, top, and at the rear of the fuselage.

The Bv 250 remained on paper mainly because the war situation made it redundant. The project could have been revived when attacks on US territory were planned, but its performance failed to match that of other bombers designed for that task.

**BV 250**
© Marek Ryś 2007

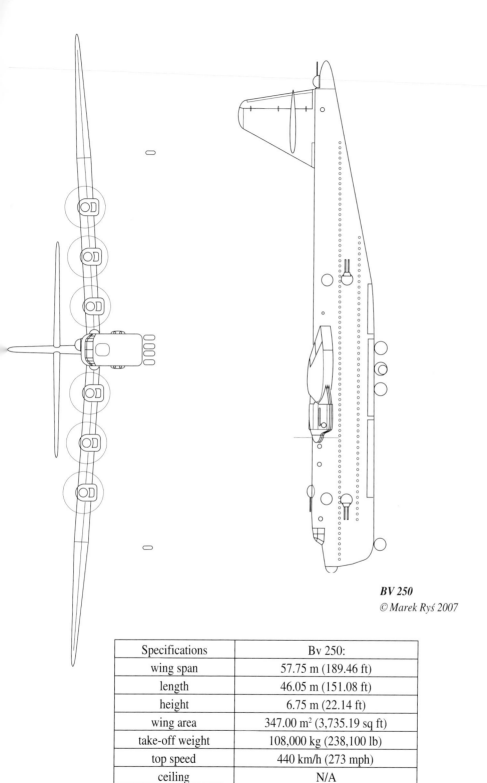

*BV 250*
© *Marek Ryś 2007*

| Specifications | Bv 250: |
|---|---|
| wing span | 57.75 m (189.46 ft) |
| length | 46.05 m (151.08 ft) |
| height | 6.75 m (22.14 ft) |
| wing area | 347.00 m² (3,735.19 sq ft) |
| take-off weight | 108,000 kg (238,100 lb) |
| top speed | 440 km/h (273 mph) |
| ceiling | N/A |
| range | 2,500-15,000 km (1,553-9,321 miles) |

# BMW

## SCHNELLBOMBER PROJECT I (A)

BMW is known mostly as a maker of engines, boBMW is known mostly as a maker of engines, both piston and jet, but they also developed aircraft projects. The bomber project is known in the literature as the Schnellbomber Project I, Project A, or the BMW Strählbomber mit PTL 028. It had a classic layout, except for its unusual wings. Their central sections were swept forward and had significant dihedral. Outer sections were swept back and had very slight dihedral. At the joint of these sections BMW 028 turbo-props rated at 6,570 hp and 5.8 kN thrust were located in narrow, long

nacelles. A 33.0 kN BMW 018 jet was mounted under its rear part. The BMW bomber was, therefore, to be powered by four engines. The BMW 028s drove eight-bladed contra-rotating propellers. The long fuselage housed the pressurised cockpit for the crew of three at the front. The fuel tank, the bomb bay and the main wheel well were located further aft. The undercarriage consisted of a four-wheel main bogie, a nose wheel and stabilising wheels retracting into the wings. The wings also housed the additional fuel tanks (for a total tankage of 29,400 litres), and bomb bays. Maximum bomb

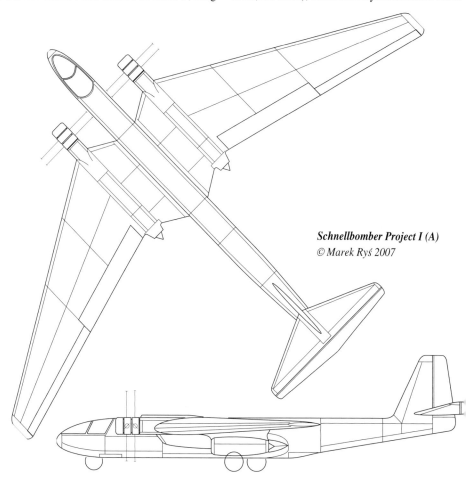

*Schnellbomber Project I (A)*
© *Marek Ryś 2007*

load would be 16,000kg, but already at 11,000kg the range fell to 2,550km (from 4,500km in clean configuration). When flown on BMW 028s alone, this figure rose to 5,200km.

Generally, long cruises would be flown using turbo-props only, while the jets were used in emergency or for fast attacks against selected targets. Aircraft armament would be located in remotely-controlled ventral and dorsal fuselage turrets.

Specifications

| | |
|---|---|
| wing span | 50.50 m (165.68 ft) |
| length | 34.60 m (113.51 ft) |
| height | 9.00 m (29.52 ft) |
| wing area | 250 m² (2,691.06 sq ft) |
| empty weight | N/A |
| take-off weight | 78,800 kg (173,724 lb) |
| top speed | 620 km/h (385 mph) (BMW 028 only) |
| | 870 km/h (540 mph)(with jet engines) |
| ceiling | 11,000 m (36,090ft) |
| range | 4,000 km (2485 miles) |

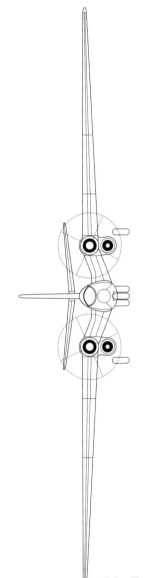

*Schnellbomber*
*Project I (A)*
© Marek Ryś 2007

# SCHNELLBOMBER
# PROJECT II (B)

This project was without a doubt one of the most unusual German designs of the war. The fuselage, identical to Project I, was fitted with forward-swept wings. The undercarriage was unchanged, but the power plant was completely altered. The additional jet engines were discarded, and the two BMW 028s were located high above the fuselage on special pylons mounted on the upper fuselage structure and angled by 45° to the sides. The unusual layout was supposed to keep the slipstream and exhaust gases away from the tail.The project was developed at the end of 1943 under Ing. Kappus.

The armament was similar to that of the Project I, but the bomb load was limited to 2,000kg.

RLM was not interested in the aircraft, but the company continued to work on it as a private venture until late in 1944.

Specifications:

| | |
|---|---|
| wing span | 32.50 m ( 106.62 ft) |
| length | 28.00 m (91.86 ft) |
| height | 6.50 m (21.32 ft) |
| top speed | 870 km/h (541 mph) |
| range | 2,800 km (1740 miles) |

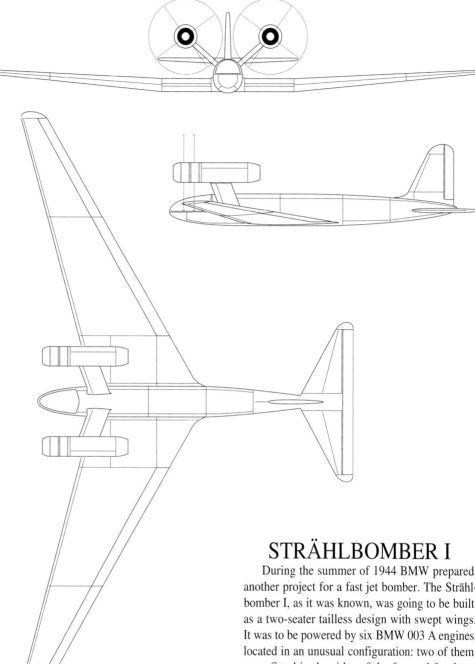

*Schnellbomber Project II (B)*
© Marek Ryś 2007

# STRÄHLBOMBER I

During the summer of 1944 BMW prepared another project for a fast jet bomber. The Strählbomber I, as it was known, was going to be built as a two-seater tailless design with swept wings. It was to be powered by six BMW 003 A engines located in an unusual configuration: two of them were fitted in the sides of the forward fuselage, under the pressurised cockpit, and another four were located in the wings, two on each wing, side-by-side with a common air intake in the leading edge. The wings also housed the fuel tanks and main wheel wells. The nose wheel well was located between the fuselage-mounted engines.

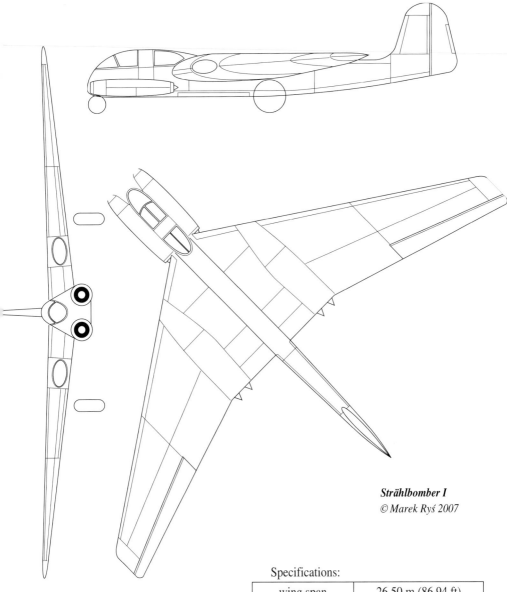

*Strählbomber I*
© *Marek Ryś 2007*

The fuselage, essentially a stretched fuselage boom, was very narrow and would not be able to house the bomb bay, so most probably the entire bomb load (5,000kg) would have had to be placed in wing bays or under the wings on external mounts. Although no information about the planned armament survives, most probably it would have been located in remotely-controlled gun positions.

Specifications:

| | |
|---|---|
| wing span | 26.50 m (86.94 ft) |
| length | 18.00 m (59.05 ft) |
| height | 4.35 m (14.27 ft) |
| wing area | 100 m² (1076.42 sq ft) |
| empty weight | N/A |
| take-off weight | 25,000 kg (55,115 lb) |
| top speed | 856 km/h (532 mph at altitude of 6,400 m |
| ceiling | N/A |
| range | 2,704 km (1680 miles) |

# STRÄHLBOMBER II

In parallel with the development of the Strähl-bomber I, the BMW design office continued work on another bomber, designated the Strählbomber II. It was an aircraft built in the flying wing layout, but with a distinctive fuselage, housing the crew of three and two BMW 018 jet engines. The remaining space was occupied by engine air ducts (intakes at the front of the fuselage). The pilot sat in the forward section of the cockpit, with the navigator/gunner further aft and facing the rear. The bomb-aimer was in a prone position in the lower fuselage.

The wing was swept and had a sufficiently thick airfoil to house the wells of the twin main wheel units, the bomb bay beside the fuselage and the fuel tanks. Defensive armament would be located in remotely controlled turrets, operated by the gunner/navigator with a periscopic sight, as his cockpit canopy did not project beyond the fuselage outline.

Main undercarriage consisted of two sets of two wheels each, mounted in tandem. They were complemented by a nose wheel which retracted into the fuselage under the cockpit.

The aircraft was going to carry 5,000 kg of bombs, reaching a range of 4,000 km. Needless to say, there was no chance to complete the project and build the prototype, and at the end of 1944 the whole programme was cancelled.

Specifications:

| | |
|---|---|
| wing span | 35.50 m (116.47 ft) |
| length | 18.00 m (59.06 ft) |
| height | 4.50 m (14.76 ft) |
| wing area | 115.70 m² (1,245.38 sq ft) |
| empty weight | N/A |
| take-off weight | 31,500 kg (68.343 lb) |
| top speed | 950 km/h (590 mph) |
| ceiling | N/A |
| range | 4,000 km (2,485 m) |

*Strählbomber II*
© Marek Ryś 2007

# DAIMLER BENZ

## 310256-05

The Daimler Benz project known as the 'A' and 'B' was one of the more unusual ideas of German aircraft engineers during the war. It will be described in more detail in the volume on special aircraft, but it is worth noting here that Projects A and B were carriers of bombers and flying bombs intended to attack US territory, and their concept resulted from an attempt to attain maximum range. In Project A a giant carrier would be used to bring a smaller bomber near the target. The bomber was known in drawings as no. 310256-05. According to some sources, it was this bomber that was going to be designated as the 'B', but most probably the letter B was to be applied to the second carrier machine (Project B), transporting piloted flying bombs.

The aircraft carried by Project A was a mid-wing monoplane with swept wings and a long, cigar-shaped fuselage. Above the fuselage the 110.45 kN DB 016 jet was located. The tail was designed in two variants: a swept tailplane with twin fins, or a V-type. The bomber was going to be delivered to the vicinity of the target by the Daimler Benz A carrier aircraft, but it was also fitted with its own, tricycle undercarriage. This retracted into the wings and fuselage. The aircraft was able to carry up to 30,000kg of bombs in different configurations (such as 60 x SC 500, 30 x SB 1,000 etc.) and it would be released at an altitude of 10,000m.

The programme of A and B carrier aircraft was prepared by Daimler Benz as a preliminary project only. Engineering and aerodynamic details were prepared by Focke Wulf designers, under Kurt Tank himself.

Specifications:

| | |
|---|---|
| wing span | 22.00 m (72.17 ft) |
| length | 30.75 m (100.88 ft) |
| height | 8.50 m (27.88 ft) |
| all-up weight | 70,000 kg (154,324 lb) |

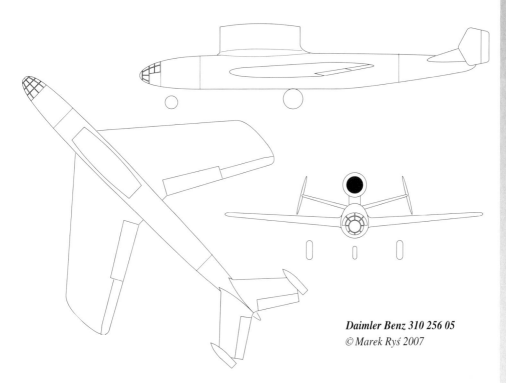

*Daimler Benz 310 256 05*
© *Marek Ryś 2007*

# FOCKE WULF

## TO (Trans Ocean)

At the end of the 1930s the TO (Trans Ocean) aircraft was under development for German airlines. Its military variant, under the preliminary designation of 'Project B' was going to be able to carry 4,000kg of bombs over 8,000 km. The machine was to be powered by four 24-cylinder 2,700 hp Daimler Benz DB 606 in-line engines. It was assumed that the new machine would replace the excellent, but ageing, Fw 200 Condor.

The bomber was a classic low-wing monoplane with straight wings and twin vertical tails. The crew of several men was able to move around the fuselage, the shape being derived from the passenger machine. The undercarriage consisted of four main wheels on separate legs, retracting into the wings, and the tail wheel retracting into the fuselage. The power plant concept was very unusual: the four DB 606 engines were located inside the fuselage, driving wing-mounted propellers via special trans-

mission gear. Externally, the machine looked like a classic four-engined aircraft.

The innovative power plant concept failed to please RLM officials, who preferred the development version designated Project F, with the engines where they would normally be, in nacelles under the wings. This had the advantage of leaving more room inside the fuselage and of improving the cooling conditions for the engines. Drag rose only slightly.

Project L had a completely redesigned fuselage. the design consisting in joining the bottom section with an upper section that had a larger diameter. This resulted in more space inside the fuselage.

The RLM received two more proposals, designated the Project R and Project S. Nothing is known about these two designs.

This programme was cancelled in 1941, as the war situation did not require this type of machine.

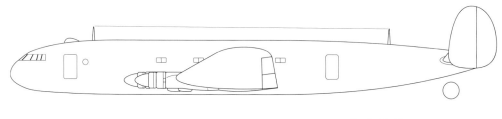

*Focke Wulf TO*
© *Marek Ryś 2007*

| Specifications | TO Project B: |
|---|---|
| wing span | 35.80 m (117.45 ft) |
| length | 28.10 m (92.19 ft) |
| height | N/A |
| wing area | 128 m² (1,377.82 sq ft) |
| take-off weight | 42,000 kg (92,594 lb) |
| top speed | 700 km/h (435 mph) |

# Fw 300

As early as 1941, Focke Wulf prepared another project for Deutsche Lufthansa, designated the Fw 300 and powered by four 2,500 hp Jumo 222 engines. In 1942 the RLM ordered its conversion to a guided missile carrier with a range of 8,800km. The aircraft was a low-wing monoplane of all-metal construction, with a crew of eight. The undercarriage, similar to that of the TO project, consisted of four main wheels on individual legs, and a tail wheel. Defensive armament, in the form of twin MG 151/20 cannon, was located in six remotely-controlled turrets. The offensive armament was going to consist of guided bombs, to be used against shipping, similar to those on the Fw 200, which the new design was intended to succeed. The plans came to nothing and aircraft remained a project only.

Specifications:

| wing span | 46.20 m (151.57 ft) |
|---|---|
| length | 37.34 m (122.50 ft) |
| height | N/A |
| wing area | 227.0 m² (2,443.48 sq ft) |
| range | 8,800 km at a speed of 530 km/h (5,468 miles at a speed of 330 mph) |

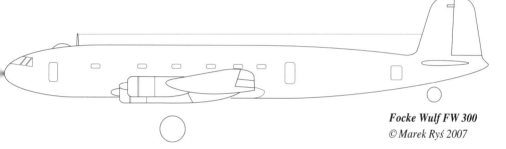

*Focke Wulf FW 300*
© *Marek Ryś 2007*

# Fw 191B/C

For the 'Bomber B' competition, announced by the RLM in July 1939, Focke Wulf submitted the twin-engined Fw 191 bomber designed by the team under Ing. Kosel. The machine, in accordance with the terms of the bid, was to be powered by Jumo 222A engines. The forward fuselage housed an extensively glazed pilot's and navigator's cockpit, and the central fuselage was occupied by the bomb bay, with fuel tanks above it. Electrically operated gun turrets were located on the fuselage, forward and aft of the bomb bay. The third gun position was located under the fuselage. Twin vertical tails were used. As the aircraft was a high-wing monoplane, the main wheel legs that retracted into the engine nacelles had to be relatively long. The tail wheel retracted into the fuselage.

This was a heavily armed aircraft: two 7.9mm MG 81 machine guns were located under the cock- pit, with two more located in remotely-controlled positions at the rear ends of the engine nacelles and another two in a turret on the fuselage. The rear turret manned by the flight engineer had a 20mm MG 151 cannon, and the ventral turret, two more MG 81s.

The RLM pressed Focke Wulf to use electric power as much as possible to actuate flaps, ailerons and turrets, instead of hydraulic systems. This was an advanced solution, but it required fitting many electric motors and providing sufficient electric power from batteries or generators. As a result, the weight of the aircraft rose significantly.

The first prototype Fw 191 V1, pattern machine for the 'A' series, was ready in 1942, unlike the Jumo 222 engines. It was, therefore, powered by much less powerful BMW 801 MAs, rated at 1,600 hp each. No great performance was expected, the

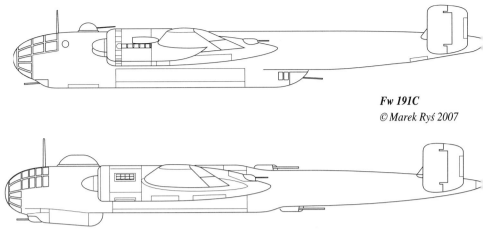

*Fw 191C*
© *Marek Ryś 2007*

*FW 191 with Jumo 222 engines*
© *Marek Ryś 2007*

point was just to get the aircraft into the air. The planned armament was not fitted, either, just mock-ups of the turrets.

The prototype was plagued by electric failures from the very beginning. They were so persistent that the V3, V4 and V5 prototypes were not completed. The Fw 191 V6, completed at the beginning of 1943, was given a hydraulic rather than an electric system. Almost at the time of the aircraft's first flights the RLM cancelled the programme because the Jumo 222 failed to reach production status. Moreover (with no reason given) work was banned on a modification with Daimler Benz DB 610A engines rated at 2,700 hp for take-off (or almost 900 hp more than the Jumo 222A). This had been planned as the power plant of the Fw 191B version that itself was also not built.

The Fw 191B was supposed to be more heavily armed than in the original project: 20mm MG 151 cannon and 13mm MG 131 machine guns would be fitted in remotely-controlled turrets, and the bomb load would be 2,000kg or even 3,000kg in an overload configuration.

The Fw 191 V13 was planned as the prototype for the Fw 191B, soon to be joined by four more prototypes, numbered V14-V18. Not one of these was built.

When work on the DB 610- or DB 606-powered Fw 191 was banned, the designers decided to try one last shot, and proposed to the Ministry

a 'low cost' variant, the Fw 191C (sometimes designated in company documents as the Fw 391 or Fw 491). The variant received a modified fuselage which, in place of the short nacelle under the cockpit, featured a long 'bathtub' from the nose back to the rear fuselage, ending at the rear ventral gun position. Turrets were manually operated. The power plant would consist of four popular, and readily-available Jumo 211A engines. The company declared that, should the Luftwaffe order the aircraft, production would start very quickly. This failed to convince ministry officials and no interest in the bomber was expressed. The company terminated all work, including any plans to use DB 605L, DB 628 or DB 614 engines.

| Specifications | Fw 191 with 2x Jumo 222: |
|---|---|
| wing span | 25.00 m (82.02 ft) |
| length | 18.45 m (60.53 ft) |
| height | 4.80 m (15.74 ft) |
| wing area | 70.50 m$^2$ (758.88 sq ft) |
| empty weight | 11,970 kg (26,390 lb) |
| take-off weight | 19,557 kg (43,116 lb) |
| top speed | 620 km/h (385 mph) at an altitude of 6350m (21,000 ft) |
| ceiling | 9,700 m (31,824 ft) |
| range | 3,600 km (2,237 miles) |

# Ta 400

The Ta 400 was one of the more advanced bomber projects from Focke Wulf. Developed at Bad Eilsen under Kurt Tank himself, the project was born in 1943 to an RLM specification for a bomber with the capacity to attack the US with a bomb load of 10,000kg. The aircraft was a high-wing monoplane of all-metal construction. The pressurised fuselage housed a cockpit at the front, followed by a long bomb bay, armament operator's compartment, fuel tanks and equipment bays. The crew consisted of nine men. The undercarriage, with a single nose wheel and four main wheels, retracted into the fuselage and engine nacelles.

Power was provided by six 1,750 hp BMW 801D fourteen-cylinder two-row radials. In one variant the two outer engines were to be boosted by 8.9 kN Junkers Jumo 004B jet engines, fitted in a common nacelle. 32 fuel tanks (12 in each wing and 8 in the fuselage) in the aircraft housed a total of 27,000 litres of fuel.

Defensive armament was to be located in remotely-controlled turrets on the spine of the fuselage, underneath the body and in the tail. It consisted of twin 30mm MK 103 cannon in the FDL 103Z turret, three twin 20mm MG 151 cannon in two HD 151Z turrets and one FDL 151Z turret, and twin 13mm MG 131 machine guns in the HL 131V position. The fuselage bomb bay could accommodate up to 10,000kg of bombs, but these could also be carried under the fuselage and engine nacelles. Typical combat load inside the fuselage was going to consist of bombs and missiles in the following configurations:

| 4 x SC 2500 | 10,000 kg (22,046.24 lb) |
|---|---|
| 4x SC 1800 | 7,200 kg (15,873.29 lb) |
| 4x SC 1000 | 4,000 kg (8,818,49 lb) |
| 2x LMF Mines | 4,400 kg (9,700.34 lb) |
| 2x Fritz X guided bomb | 1,952 kg (4,303.42 lb) |
| 9x SD 1000 | 9,000 kg (19,841.61 lb) |
| 12x SD 500 E | 6,000 kg (13,227.74 lb) |

The racks under the engine nacelles could carry:

| 2x SC 2500 | 5,000 kg (11,023.12 lb) |
|---|---|
| 2x SC 1800 | 3,600 kg (7,936.64 lb) |
| 2x SC 1000 | 2,000 kg (4,409.24 lb) |
| 2x SD 1000 | 2,000 kg (4,409.24 lb) |
| 2x naval mine | 4,400 kg (9,700.34 lb) |
| 2x Hs 294 | 4,400 kg (9,700.34 lb) |
| 2x Hs 293 | 3,100 kg (6,834.33 lb) |
| 2x Fritz X | 1,952 kg (4,303.42 lb) |

One 2,200kg Hs 294 radio-controlled rocket missile or two 1,952kg Hs 293s could be carried under the fuselage.

Range of the aircraft was planned to reach 9,000 km, and the top speed was expected to be 720 km/h (when jet engines were added). As Focke Wulf was burdened with fighter contracts, the Ta 400 development programme was transferred to France, to the former SNCASO works at Chatillon sur Bagneux, near Paris. Over 300 French engineers and technicians were employed, and Italians also worked on it there, tasked with designing some components.

Two versions of the forward fuselage were designed. One called for a common cockpit with glazed nose, the other – probably the final one – featured a standard cockpit with separate canopies for the pilots and for the bomb-aimer. The Ta 400 programme had very low priority, so the work continued slowly, but without major breaks. A number of wind-tunnel models were made and tested.

At the end of 1944, the entire project was cancelled. By that time only a mock-up of the forward fuselage and some components had been completed.

Specifications:

| wing span | 45.80 m (150.26 ft) |
|---|---|
| length | 28.70 m (94.16 ft) |
| height | 6.5 m (21.32 ft) |
| wing area | 170.20 m² (1,832.07 sq ft) |
| empty weight | 30,820 kg (67,946.52 lb) |
| take-off weight | 62,500 kg (137790 lb) |
| top speed ceiling | 535km/h (333) mph at an altitude of 5,700 m (18,700 ft) |
| range | 9,000 km (5592 miles) |

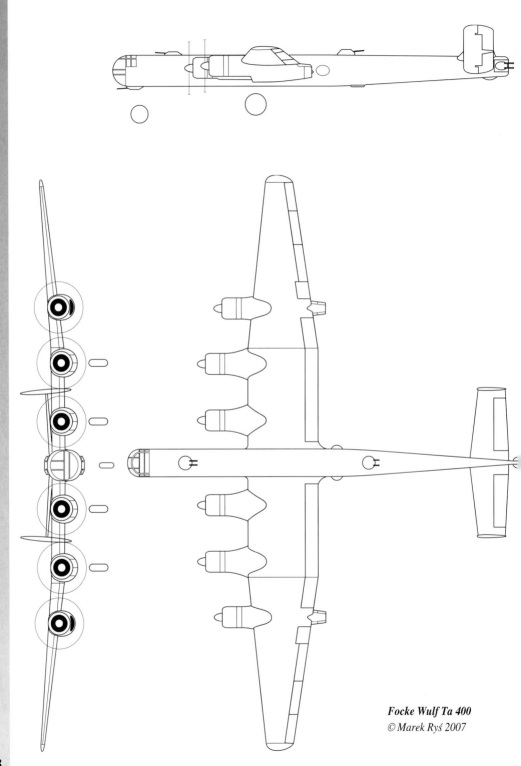

*Focke Wulf Ta 400*
© *Marek Ryś 2007*

# 1000x1000x1000 SERIES

In 1944, Focke Wulf prepared projects for three bombers, known under the designation 1000x1000x1000. Each of them was going to be powered by two Heinkel Hirth HeS 011A jet engines, and their development was supervised by Ing. H. von Halem and Ing. D. Küchemann. The name was derived from the specification for the machines: designed to carry 1,000kg of bombs over 1,000km at a speed of 1,000km/h.

The first of these aircraft, known as the 0310239-01 (or Project A), was a conventional mid-wing monoplane. The wings were swept (42° near the fuselage, 35° outboard of the engine nacelles) with the engines mounted under the main planes. The long fuselage featured a characteristic waisting, seen many years later in several post-war jets as the implementation of the 'area rule'. The tail was also swept, and the aircraft was a single-seater. It had a tandem style undercarriage that retracted into the fuselage. This was supported by two stabilising wheels, retracting into wells in the wings between the engine nacelles and the fuselage.

The aerodynamic form was a result of the requirement to reach speeds near 0.9 Mach. This necessitated suitable wing airfoil adjustment and the application of fuselage waisting. The aircraft featured an internal bomb bay, and no defensive armament was planned — the speed was supposed to make the machine immune to interception. The entire fuel load was carried in the fuselage.

The second project differed significantly, and is known as the 0310239-10 (Project B). This aircraft was designed as a flying wing with small fins and rudders at the outboard tips (in fact downward-angled wing tips). The sweep was 45°. The wing housed all of the systems and equipment, with only the cockpit protruding from the leading edge.

*Fw 0310239-10*
*© Marek Ryś 2007*

The tricycle undercarriage was retractable, and two HeS 011A engines were located inside the wing, their nozzles placed on its upper surface. Engine air intakes were located in the leading edge. Like the previous project, the aircraft had no defensive armament, and the bomb bay could house 1,000kg of bombs.

The least-known and rarely examined Project C was similar to Project A, but it was a mid-wing monoplane. It featured a fuselage carried higher off the ground, while its tail sweep angle was the same as that of the wing. The cockpit was also different - and significantly larger. Engines were mounted under the wings, but were angled inwards towards the fuselage from the centreline. This was supposed to improve the flying characteristics of the machine and to give more control over the power plant operation. This bomber again had a bomb bay and no defensive armament.

Some works mention the designation of Fw 239 for the 1000x1000x1000, but this is not corroborated by original documents. '239' was just a fragment of the drawing number. All three bombers were under development until the end of the war.

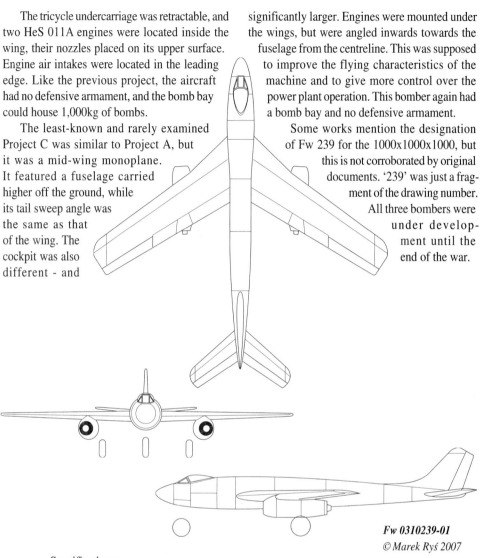

*Fw 0310239-01*
© *Marek Ryś 2007*

Specifications:

| version | Project A | Project B | Project C |
|---|---|---|---|
| wing span (m) | 12.65 (41.50 ft) | 14.00 (45.93 ft) | 12.65 (41.50 ft) |
| length (m) | 14.20 (46.58 ft) | 10.50 (34.44 ft) | 14.20 (46.58 ft) |
| height (m) | 3.75 (12.30 ft) | 2.75 (9.02 ft) | N/A |
| wing area (m²) | 27.00 (290.63 sq ft) | 55.00 (592.03 sq ft) | N/A |
| empty weight (kg) | 4,225 (9,315 lb) | 4,200 (9,259.42 lb) | N/A |
| take-off weight (kg) | 8,100 (17,857 lb) | 8,100 (17,857.45 lb) | N/A |
| top speed (km/h) at an altitude of (m) | 1,015 (631 mph) 10,000 (32,810 ft) | 1,060 (659 mph) | 1,000 (622 mph) |
| ceiling (m) | 13,500 (44,290 ft) | 14,000 (46,000 ft ) | N/A |
| range (km) | 2,500 (1,553 miles) | 2,500 (1553 miles) | N/A |

# 0310225 (Fw 261)

The bomber (identified within the company as the Fw 261, known from the drawing as no. 0310225) was intended to supersede the Fw 200. Its tasks would include maritime patrols far from the coast, anti-shipping attacks and reconnaissance support for U-boats. The aircraft was a high-wing monoplane with twin tail booms. The long fuselage nacelle housed a cockpit for the crew of seven, the armament bay, and the fuel tanks. The armament consisted of two 30mm MK 108 cannon in the nose, twin MG 151 cannon in the HD 151Z turret on top of the fuselage, two such cannon in the FDL 151Z turret under the fuselage, and four MK 108s in the tail.

The Fw 261 was planned to be powered by four BMW 801D engines rated at 1,700hp for take-off, located in nacelles under the wings. The outer nacelles extended into tail booms with vertical tails at the end. Horizontal tailplanes were mounted on the outboard side of the booms.

The bomber was going to have an endurance of up to 22 hours, and with a load of 10,000kg of bombs it would be able to reach 9,000km.

Specifications:

| | |
|---|---|
| wing span | 40.00 m (131.23 ft) |
| length | 26.10 m (85.62 ft) |
| height | 6.00 m (19.68 ft) |
| wing area | 187 m² (2,012.91 sq ft) |
| empty weight | 26,760 kg (58,995 lb) |
| take-off weight | 53,500 kg (117,947 lb) |
| top speed | 560 km/h (348 mph)  at an altitude of 7,200 m (23,622 ft) |
| ceiling | 9,600 m (31,500 ft ) |
| range | 9,000 km (5,600 miles |

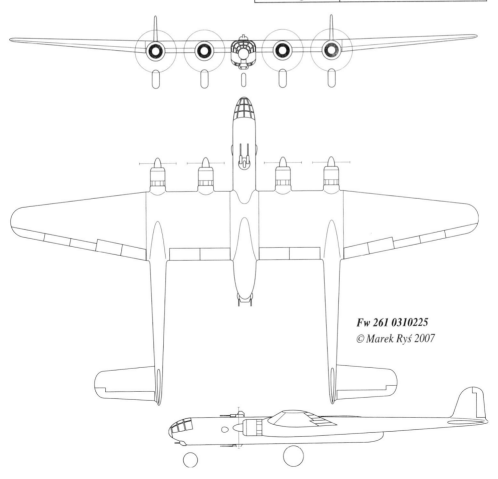

*Fw 261 0310225*
*© Marek Ryś 2007*

# Fw 238 —03.10206 SERIES

Over two years, from 1942 to 1944, Focke Wulf design offices produced a whole series of preliminary drafts of an advanced long-range bomber. Their common feature was that the fuselage of circular cross-section had an extensively glazed cockpit at the front, flush with the general aerodynamic shape of the fuselage, the latter mostly made of wood. Essentially, these looked like the Boeing B-29, but were only conincidentally similar designs. They were planned as B-29 equivalents. The interest of the RLM (little as it was) in these projects was due to the fact that the bombers would be capable to reaching the USA with a full bomb load (10,000kg), dropping their load and returning -- thanks to in-flight refuelling.

The team that developed these aircraft was led by Ing. Bansemier, Kosel, and Kurt Tank himself. On 16 July, 1942 the first bomber, known by its drawing number 03.10206-20 (or under the company designation of Fw 238) was presented to the RLM. It was powered by four 28-cylinder 4,000hp BMW 803 radials driving contra-rotating eight-bladed propellers. The crew was ten members (some sources quote five) and the total fuel load in wing- and fuselage-mounted tanks was 35,000 litres. The range, depending on the load and the engine type, reached 8,500-10,300km. The bomber was to be fitted with an in-flight refuelling system. A conventional tail wheel undercarriage included twin main wheels which retracted into the engine nacelles or wings.

Two remotely-controlled gun turrets with twin MG 151 cannon were located on top of the rear fuselage, and two similar turrets were located under the rear fuselage. The plan was to fit a gun pod under the cockpit as well, with four 30mm cannon for anti-shipping duties.

Focke Wulf representatives ensured that if ordered into production, the machine could enter service in 1944. Three principal variants were planned:

- Project A - identical with no. 03.10206-20 as presented to the RLM
- Project B - powered by four Jumo 222 C/D engines rated for 3,000 hp at take-off
- Project C - powered by six Jumo 213F or DB 603A engines rated at 1,950hp

Apart from these three variants, the design team also considered using four 2,800 hp BMW 802 two-row radials. Some sources claim that this idea was known unofficially as the Fw 238H.

Oddly, surviving drawings suggest that there were two versions of the fuselage. One was on long and slim, with a relatively small cross-section, and the other was more stubby, and shorter.

Work on the 03.10206-20 was terminated by the RLM on 14 February 1943, when instruction was issued to stop work on new bombers for the Luftwaffe and to concentrate on fighters.

| Specifications: | Fw 238 |
|---|---|
| wing span | 50.00 m (164.04 ft) |
| length | 29.70 m (97.44 ft) |
| height | 5.60 m (18.37 ft ) |
| wing area | 250 m² (2,691.06 sq ft ) |
| take-off weight | 80,500 kg (177,472 lb) |
| top spee | 550 km/h (342 mph) at an altitude of 9,500 m (31,000 ft) |
| range | 8,500-10,300 km (5,300-6,400 miles) |

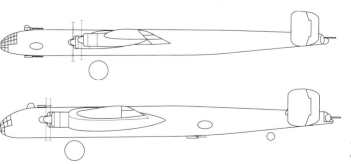

*Focke Wulf 03.10206-27*

*Focke Wulf 03.10206-22*
© *Marek Ryś 2007*

# 03.10206-22/ -27

The Fw 238 was intended to be a very large aircraft, but Focke Wulf planned to build even larger giants. By scaling up the 03.10206-20, they arrived at a bomber with a span of 63.00m! It was going to be powered by BMW 803 engines and to carry 4,000kg of bombs over a distance of 13,000km. Armament and equipment were virtually the same as its predecessor. This aircraft is known from the drawing no. 03.10206-22. That in no. 03.10206-27 was almost identical, but powered by six Jumo 222 engines, and had a different, four-wheel main undercarriage, retracting into the engine nacelles and not into the wings (as in the previous version).

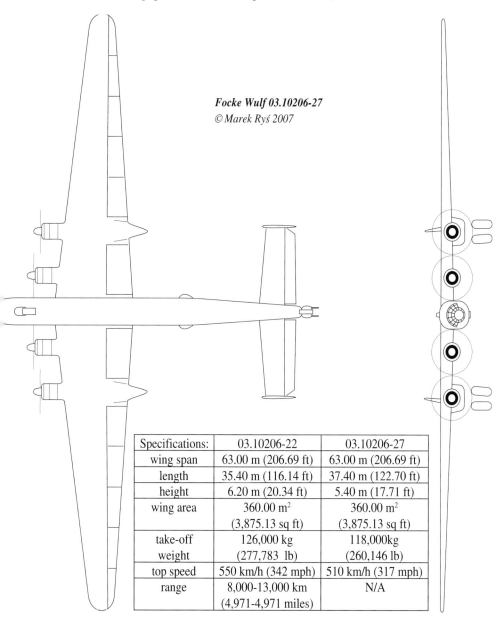

*Focke Wulf 03.10206-27*
© *Marek Ryś 2007*

| Specifications: | 03.10206-22 | 03.10206-27 |
|---|---|---|
| wing span | 63.00 m (206.69 ft) | 63.00 m (206.69 ft) |
| length | 35.40 m (116.14 ft) | 37.40 m (122.70 ft) |
| height | 6.20 m (20.34 ft) | 5.40 m (17.71 ft) |
| wing area | 360.00 m² (3,875.13 sq ft) | 360.00 m² (3,875.13 sq ft) |
| take-off weight | 126,000 kg (277,783 lb) | 118,000kg (260,146 lb) |
| top speed | 550 km/h (342 mph) | 510 km/h (317 mph) |
| range | 8,000-13,000 km (4,971-4,971 miles) | N/A |

# HEINKEL

## He 177 variants

Heinkel's He 177 was the only attempt to build a strategic bomber for the Luftwaffe that managed to reach production and operational use. However, the aircraft was a failure, mainly due to the 24-cylinder DB 610 and DB 613 power plant that had been selected. Essentially, the engines were coupled pairs of 12-cylinder units. The DB 610 was a pair of DB 601s, and the DB 613 was a twin set of DB 603 Gs. They offered great power output, but were very difficult to cool. Most He 177 failures during trial and operational use resulted from overheated engines.

The last version (only ever built as prototypes) was the high altitude He 177A-7. It was fitted with wings with a span 4.56 m longer than the production aircraft and with DB 613 engines rated at 3,600hp for take-off and 3,150hp at operational altitude. To speed up production of the new version, complete A-5 fuselages was used and six aircraft were built and fitted with the DB 610 engines. No time was left to build the 'true' A-7. At least two preliminary project versions of the aircraft are known. In both, the cockpit canopy was in the shape planned for the A-6/R2 version. The first variant featured the remotely-controlled FDL 131Z turret with twin MG 131 machine guns in the 'chin' immediately below the glazing, a dorsal remotely-controlled turret of the same type, and the HDL 81V turret with four MG 81s in the tail. One MG 131 gun was fitted in the rear section of the under-fuselage nacelle. In another variant the latter was abandoned and the FDL 131Z turret was fitted under the fuselage aft of the nacelle. The FDL 151Z with two MG 151/20 cannon was fitted at the front of the nacelle. In both cases the power plant would consist of DB 610 engines, and ultimately DB 613s.

In the other variant of the He 177A-7 design, the engines were located lower, being under the wings and their nacelles were significantly larger. This allowed the designers to introduce a new undercarriage that retracted rearwards into the engine nacelles, not sideways into the wings. The main undercarriage had twin-wheel bogies on a single leg.

Even at an early stage of development, the Japanese expressed an interest producing the He 177. They intended to acquire a licence for the aircraft and to build it at the Chiba factory owned by Hitachi. To solve the problem of overheating engines they intended to use four separately mounted radials.

A German submarine brought part of the documentation and some components to Japan. The third provisional He 177A-7, offered to the Japanese as a pattern example, was going to fly there under its own power. To this end additional fuel tanks were fitted in every available space, including the bomb bays. To reduce weight, most of the armour was removed. The Japanese, impressed with the enormous range of the aircraft, planned to use it for suicide attacks against the US coast.

Subsequent variants of the Greif failed to reach the stage of even 'provisional' prototypes. These included, among others, the He 177A-8 and A-10 with four BMW 801E radials or two DB 613 engines.

| Specifications | He 177A-7: |
|---|---|
| wing span | 36.00 m (118.11 ft) |
| length | 21.90 m (71.85 ft) |
| height | 6.40 m (20.99 ft ) |
| wing area | 102.00 m² (1,097.95 sq ft) |
| empty weight | 15,400 kg (33,951 lb) |
| max. take-off weight | 34,600 kg (76,280 lb) |
| top speed at an altitude of 6100 m | 539 km/h (335 mph) |

# He 277

The He 177's engine problems were so severe that it was eventually accepted that the only cure was to separate the engines and to fit individual nacelles. This increased drag, but significantly improved the cooling. Such a solution was proposed by Heinkel to the RLM for the prototype He 274 (He 177H) and for the new version designated the He 277.

The Ministry, however, tended to avoid development of four-engined bombers at all costs, because fighters were more imoprtant, so Heinkel's concept failed to find approval there. Nevertheless, the designer decided to develop his idea even without support from the Ministry. The He 177 with four engines in separate nacelles would be officially designated the He 177B, as the planned He 277 name could not be used without the RLM's consent, which the Ministry did not issue. As a result, both of these names are used for the same aircraft in the literature. It was not until 1943 that the aircraft found approval and could be officially named He 277, and construction of the prototype started.

The first He 277B-5/He 177B-5 was built by conversion of a production He 177A-5. It differed little from the He 177A-5, other than by having separate 1,750hp DB 603E engines and a pres-surised cockpit. It was soon found that four engines created new turbulence on the tail, and reduced the stability of the bomber. Several tail configurations were wind-tunnel tested before the twin fin-rudder layout was chosen.

The second prototype, pattern aircraft for the production He 277B-5, was apparently completed and test flown in April 1944 at Rechlin. It had an entirely new cockpit, with the canopy protruding beyond the fuselage outline, but still with a completely glazed nose. In subsequent projects the nose glazing changed several more times. Defensive armament consisted of four MG 81 guns in the forward fuselage under the cockpit, four MG 151 cannon in dorsal and ventral turrets, and four MG 131 machine guns in the tail. All of the turrets were remotely controlled.

Apart from the DB 603E-powered variant, Heinkel also planned to build a version with BMW 801 radials, and the He 277B-6 with Jumo 213 F engines. The He 277B-7 was going to have 24-cylinder Jumo 222As. The He 277 programme was cancelled on 3 July 1944. All work had to be terminated and all the components and assemblies were scrapped.

| Specifications: | He 277B-5 |
|---|---|
| wing span | 40.00m (131.23 ft) |
| length | 23.00m (75.45 ft) |
| height | 3.10m (10.17 ft) |
| wing area | N/A |
| empty weight | N/A |
| max. take-off weight | 44,000 kg (97,003 lb) |
| range | 8,000 km (4,971 miles) |

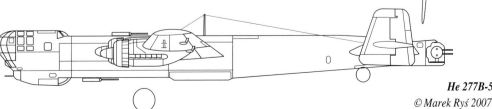

*He 277B-5*
*© Marek Ryś 2007*

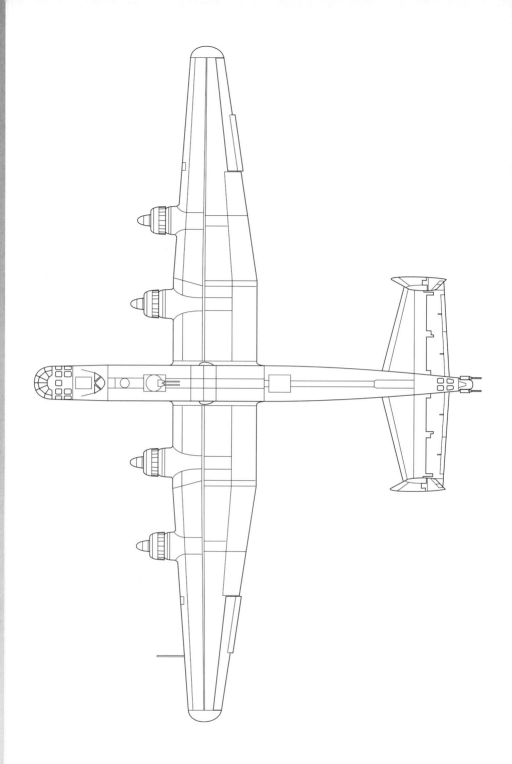

*He 277B-5*
© *Marek Ryś 2007*

# He 343/P 1068

The most promising Heinkel project which was, oddly, approved by the RLM, was the He 343 bomber developed in cooperation with Arado. It was a far-reaching development of the Arado Ar 234, scaled-up by a ratio of 1.55. Known initially as the Strählbomber mit 16to. Abfluggewicht (Strabo 16), it was an all-metal, single-seat mid-wing monoplane with tricycle undercarriage and a pressurised cockpit. The fuselage housed the cockpit, bomb bay and fuel tanks. Wings were straight, as was the tail. The undercarriage retracted into the fuselage.

Four HeS 011A engines were fitted in separate nacelles under the wings. The designers also planned to use Jumo 004B and Jumo 012 engines. The armament was going to consist of two rearward-firing 20mm MG 151 cannon located in the lower rear fuselage. The RLM also required a tail turret. The bomb load was 3,000kg.

Slightly later, two more variants of the He 343 were developed: the He 343A-3 Zerstörer with twin vertical tails and a turret with MG 151 cannon in the tail, and the He 343A-2 reconnaissance machine.

At the same time as work progressed on the approved versions, further, parallel development of the aircraft continued under the designation P.1068. It was requested, in November 1944, that the aircraft should be able to carry the Fritz X guided bomb. In the first variant (P.1068.80) the power plant was going to consist of six HeS 011A or Jumo 004C engines located in nacelles under the wings. In the P.1068.82 it was planned to place the engines in clusters of three in common nacelles. The last variant, P.1068.84 of 14 January

1945, had a completely new swept wing and four HeS 011A engines located in an unusual position. Two of these were located forward underneath the wing roots and the other two over the wings at the root immediately forward of the trailing edge. A swept horizontal tail was also included.

In November 1943 a complete description of the P.1068/He 343 project was delivered to RLM officials. Heinkel hit the right moment, as Hitler was in his 'bomber phase' and demanded accelerated work on jet bombers. Several companies were ordered to do such work, and prototypes were required no later than April 1945. Three more were to be ready by May, and five aircraft of the A-0 batch were required in June 1945. As Heinkel was well advanced in work on the P.1068 in February 1944, it was decided to increase the number of aircraft on order to ten. In March 1944 the wooden mock-up of the airframe was completed.

Planned aircraft designs were tested on free flying models, as well as wind-tunnel models. The wind tunnel models were made by Schmetz company in April 1944 and the tests were carried out in a centre belonging to the DFS company at Hörsching, near Linz (Austria).

The situation of the aircraft industry and the unpredictable caprices of Hitler and the RLM inspired Heinkel to work as quickly as possible, before the authorities changed their minds. An additional spur was provided in the form of the Junkers Ju 287.

On 22 June, 1944 a time schedule of the work was prepared, plus a list of

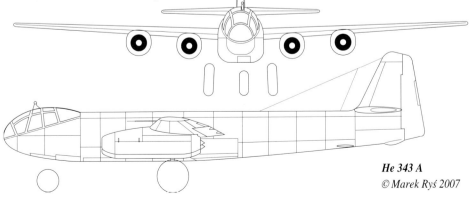

*He 343 A*
© *Marek Ryś 2007*

the planned twenty prototype aircraft, as follows:

- He 343 V1 (W.Nr. 850061) — the first prototype; two-seater variant
- He 343 V2 (W.Nr. 850062) — the second prototype for engine tests and flying trials
- He 343 V3 (W.Nr. 850063) — the third prototype for armament tests
- He 343 V4 (W.Nr. 850064) — three-seater variant
- He 343 V5 (W.Nr. 850065) — high altitude and long range tests; reconnaissance variant
- He 343 V6 (W.Nr. 850066) — wooden wings, plastic tail; Zerstörer variant
- He 343 V7-V20 (W.Nr. 850067-850080) — different Zerstörer variants, with varying armament.

On 16 July, 1944 Ing. Hart, in charge of the work, was notified by the RLM that the order was reduced to two test aircraft. These were cancelled, too, when in August 1944

**He 343 A**
© Marek Ryś 2007

all effort was switched to fighters. The Jägerstab ordered scrapping of all the prepared components, but this was not done. Complete sub-assemblies for the V1 and V2 were stored. They were eventually destroyed following a renewed order in November 1944.

| Version | P.1068.78 | P.1068.80 | P.1068.83 | P.1068.84 | He 343A-1 |
|---|---|---|---|---|---|
| Wing span | 19 m (62.33 ft) | 19m (62.33 ft) | 17 m (55.77 ft) | 17 m (55.77 ft) | 18 m (59.05 ft) |
| Length | 20 m (65.61 ft) | 20 m (65.61 ft) | 17 m (55.77 ft) | 17 m (55.77 ft ) | 16 m (54.13 ft) |
| Height | 2.10 m (6.88 ft) | 2.10 m (6.88 ft) | 1.80 m (5.90 ft) | 1.80 m (5.90 ft) | 5.35 m (17.55 ft) |
| Wing area | 60.00 m² (645.85 sq ft) | 60.00 m² (645.85 sq ft) | 43.00 m² (462.86 sq ft) | 45.00 m² (484.39 sq ft) | 42.25 m² (454.79 sq ft) |
| Empty weight | 12,830 kg (28,285 lb) | 14,800 kg (32,628 lb) | 10,760 kg (23,722 lb) | 11,060 kg (24,383 lb) | 5,260 kg (11,596 lb) |
| Take-off weight | 22,300 kg (49,163 lb) | 23,500 kg (51,809 lb) | 17,960 kg (39,595 lb) | 18,260 kg (40,256 lb) | 17,945 kg (39,561 lb) |
| Top speed | 853 km/h (530 mph) at an altitude of 6000m (19,685ft) | 930 km/h (578 mph) | 910 km/h (566 mph) | 895 km/h (556 mph) at an altitude of 6000m (20,000 ft) | 835 km/h (519 mph) at an altitude of 6000m (20,000 ft) |
| Ceiling | 11,000 m (36,100 ft) | 13,200 m (43,307 ft) | 12,700 m (41,667 ft) | 12,500 m (41,000 ft) | 10,000 m (32,808 ft) |
| Range | 2,220 km (1,379 miles) | 1,430 km (889 miles) | 1,670 km (1,038 miles) | 1,620 km (1,007 miles) | 1,620 km (1,007 miles) |

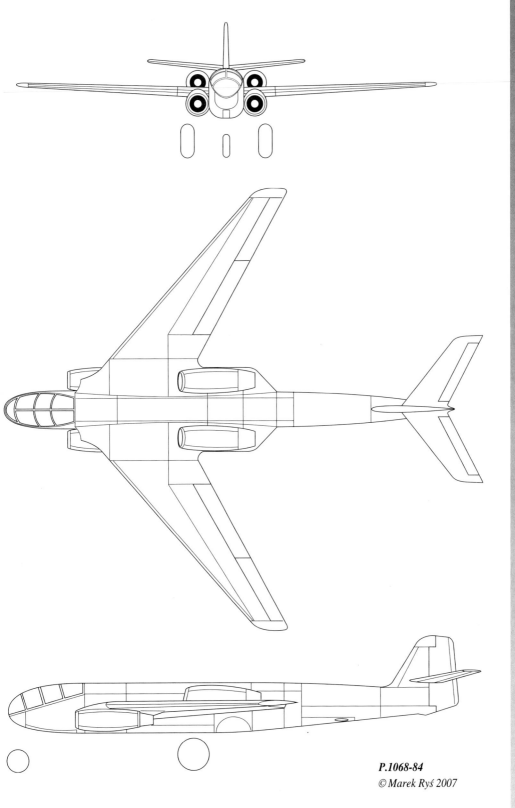

*P.1068-84*
© *Marek Ryś 2007*

# P.1065.01-IIIb/IIIc

In June 1942, the RLM issued a specification for an army cooperation aircraft, which was intended to replace the Bf 110, Ju 88 and Ju 188. Heinkel was one of the companies who entered the bid, submitting their P.1065 project. Assault and Zerstörer variants were planned, but in this book we are only interested in the third version of the machine, a fast bomber, designated in the literature as the P.1065-IIIb. Its concept was very similar to the He 119 (built) and the P.1055.01-16 project.

The plan was to place two of the crew at the front of the fuselage in an extensively glazed cockpit, and the 4,540hp 28-cylinder DB 619 engine (a coupled pair of DB 609s) in the fuselage immediately aft of it. The four-bladed propeller was located forward of the cockpit, so the drive shaft passed right through the middle of the cabin. The rest of the fuselage was occupied by fuel tanks and equipment, so bombs would have to be carried on racks under the fuselage and wings. Defensive armament was limited to two 20mm MG 151 cannon in a remotely controlled position in the tail of the machine. The armament operator's compartment (the armament operator being the third crew member) was going to be located under a glass dome in the rear fuselage immediately aft of the wing trailing edge.

The wing had a tapered planform and the classic tail included a single fin and tailplanes, although a variant with twin fins was also planned. A tail wheel undercarriage was retracted into the wings (main) and fuselage (tailwheel).

Heinkel's proposal met little interest from the RLM, and in addition there was also some personal animosity between the designer and some officials, so the P1065 remained on paper.

There were few variants of this project, differed in general layout. Sometimes differences were radical. Some of this variants are presented on published drawings.

Specifications:

| wing span | 20.30 m (66.60 ft) |
|---|---|
| length | 14.40 m (47.24 ft) |
| height | N/A |
| wing area | 45.00 m² (484.39 sq ft) |
| empty weight | N/A |
| max. take-off weight | 14,870 kg (32,782 lb) |
| top speed | 560 km/h (348 mph) |
| ceiling | N/A |
| range | N/A |

There were a few variants of this project, differed in general layout. Sometimes differences were radical. Some of this variants are presented on published drawings.

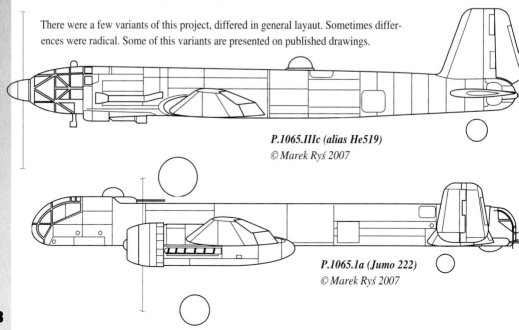

*P.1065.IIIc (alias He519)*
© Marek Ryś 2007

*P.1065.1a (Jumo 222)*
© Marek Ryś 2007

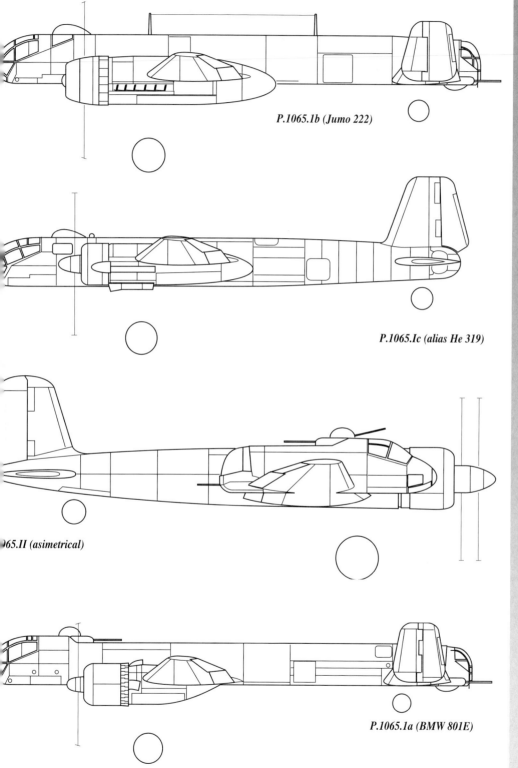

*P.1065.1b (Jumo 222)*

*P.1065.Ic (alias He 319)*

*)65.II (asimetrical)*

*P.1065.1a (BMW 801E)*

# LONG RANGE BOMBER

After the war, when US officers questioned members of the Heinkel design team, their testimonies and reports included information about a long range bomber that was in development until May 1945. It was to have swept wings (the sweep changing along the leading edge from 35° to 45°) and it would have been powered by four HeS 011A engines buried completely in the wings.

In reconstructions of the design the long range bomber showed a marked similarity to the later British 'V' bombers. Another version was a flying wing powered by BMW 018 or six Jumo 004D engines. The take-off weight of the latter was going to reach 60,000kg, including a bomb load of 3,000kg. Most of the weight was fuel, allowing it to achieve a range of 28,000km. According to the testimony of Ing. Siegfried Günther, the aircraft was developed in response to the results of the conference at Dessau, in which Göring participated, on 22 February 1945. It is difficult to ascertain now if this

work was really done, or if Günther simply wanted to increase his importance in the perception of the Allies.

## Specifications

| wing span | 31.50 m (103.34 ft) |
|---|---|
| length | 19.85 m (65.12 ft) |
| range | 28,000 km (17,398 miles) |

*Heinkel 60-ton bomber*
*© Marek Ryś 2007*

# HENSCHEL

## P.122

The Henschel project designated P.122 was an aircraft that could easily be imagined as either a bomber or a Zerstörer aircraft. However, its capabilities were more typical for a classic bomber than for a Zerstörer. Thus it was categorised as a high altitude bomber in the Allied report following their interrogation of the Henschel designers and analysis of captured documents.

The first information about the P.122 reached the RLM at the beginning of 1945, and attained top secret status. The aircraft was a twin-engined, all-metal tailless low-wing monoplane with swept wings. The crew of two was located at the front, in a pressurised cockpit. Two BMW 018 engines rated at 34 kN thrust each were located in nacelles under the wings. The tricycle undercarriage retracted into the fuselage.

Little can be said about the armament of the machine, as it is not clear if the fuselage housed a bomb bay or not. There are reasons to believe that the P.122 was going to carry Hs 293, Hs 294 and Hs 295 guided missiles.

The machine is still subject to controversy. Some authors believe it was a fighter; some an attack aircraft. Oddly, none of the surviving project drawings shows any offensive armament.

Specifications:

| | |
|---|---|
| wing span | 22.40 m (73.49 ft) |
| length | 12.40 m (40.68 ft) |
| height | 5.90 m (19.36 ft) |
| wing area | 70.00 m$^2$ (753.47 sq ft) |
| empty weight | N/A |
| max. take-off weight | 15,100 kg (33,290 lb) |
| top speed | 1,100 km/h (684 mph) |
| ceiling | 17,000 m (55,774 ft) |
| range | 2,000 km (1,243 mi) |

*Henschel P.122*
*© Marek Ryś 2007*

# HORTEN

# Ho XVIII

The Horten brothers, enfants terribles of the German aircraft industry and enthusiasts of the flying wing layout, did not follow the appropriate process for their projects from an official point of view. For example, the Ho 229 fighter was concealed from RLM officials for a long time, but after the prototype was first flown successfully, the RLM ordered nine more of the aircraft to be built in the Gotha and Klemm factories, with an option to expand the order to normal production.

The brothers no longer had to worry about lack of funding and materials, and Knemeyer* had another, very tempting offer for them. He asked the Hortens to design a jet powered bomber able to reach the USA with a load of 1,000kg bombs and to return without refuelling. The brothers agreed, declaring that preliminary calculations on the project would be ready within 10 days. This was to be undertaken in complete secrecy.

The Hortens' recipe to bomb USA was, unsurprisingly, a flying wing. The first project, designated the Ho XVIIIA (or Ho 18A), had many similarities to the Ho 229. It was a bomber with a clean flying wing layout; the engines were located inside the wing centre section with exhaust nozzles on its upper surface, and they were either six Jumo 004H jet engines rated at 11 kN thrust, or HeS 011A jet engines. The cockpit was located at the front, and, probably, so were the remotely-controlled turrets with defensive armament (30 mm MK 213 cannon). The tricycle undercarriage retracted into the 'fuselage/wing', and the main undercarriage units were probably fitted with multiple wheels. The bomb bay could house up to 5,000kg of bombs.

Clean aerodynamic lines and the capacity to carry a large amount of fuel promised a range of some 11,000km. The proposed variant was without

a doubt very innovative, but it would be complicated to produce. The Hortens therefore offered another, simpler model, designated the Ho XVIIIB (Ho 18B), in at least two phases. The first one is known as the Ho XVIIIB-1 and combined the wings of the Ho XVIIIA (without the engines) with the unusual eight-wheel undercarriage. Wheels (in sets of four) were located in tandem on a special system of legs, and the whole was covered with huge spats, enclosed at the bottom after take-off. Four HeS 011A jet engines were mounted at the joint of the spat with the wing. In the first project they were lower than the wings, while in the second they were partly buried in the bottom surface of the wings.

There was also a variant that was going to be powered with piston engines located in the rear part of the wing centre section, driving two sets of contra-rotating eight-bladed propellers.

The second version, known as the Ho XVIIIB-2, was a completely different aircraft, with its own classic tricycle undercarriage retracting into the wings. The aircraft was a compromise between the pure flying wing layout and the advantages of a fin. The latter was rather unusual, as it blended into the fuselage, which, in side view, had a triangular shape. The front of the 'triangle' housed the cockpit, while the rear section was the rudder. Remotely-controlled gun positions with MG 151 cannon were located at the front or the rear of the aircraft. Four Jumo 004H jet engines were located in pairs housed in two cowlings under the wing centre section.

On 23 March 1945 Göring, delighted with their idea, awarded the Hortens with a contract for a prototype. Assembly was going to start on 1 April 1945 in the underground Kahla factory in Thuringen. Needless to say, nothing came of these plans.

---

* See page 5

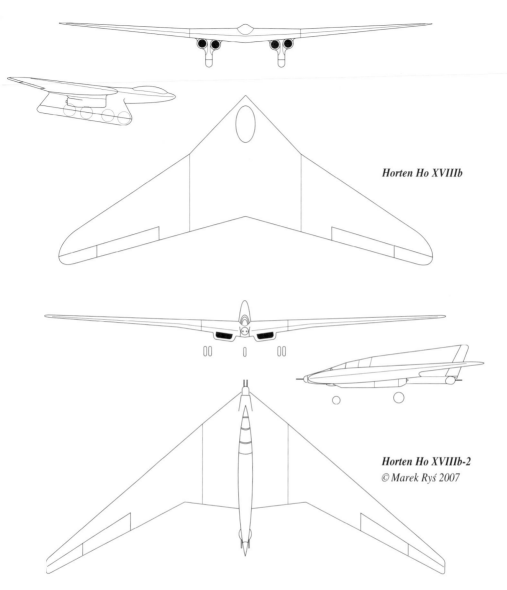

*Horten Ho XVIIIb*

*Horten Ho XVIIIb-2*
© *Marek Ryś 2007*

| Specifications: | Ho XVIIIA | Ho XVIIIB-1 | Ho XVIIIB-2 |
|---|---|---|---|
| wing span | 40.00m (131.23 ft) | 30.00m (98.42 ft) | 42.50m (139.43 ft) |
| length | 19.00m (62.33 ft) | N/A | N/A |
| height | 5.80m (19.02 ft) | 5.80m (19.02 ft) | N/A |
| wing area | 150.00m² (1,614.63 sq ft) | 156.00m² (1,679.22 sq ft) | N/A |
| empty weight | 11,000kg (24,250 lb) | 18,144kg (40,000 lb) | N/A |
| take-off weight | 32,000kg (70,548 lb) | 33,112kg (73.000 lb) | 41,800kg (92,153 lb) |
| top speed | 900km/h (559 mph) | 860km/h (534 mph) | 910km/h (566 mph) |
| ceiling | N/A | N/A | N/A |
| range | 11,000km (6,835 miles) | 6,580km (4,089 miles) | 9,000-12,000km (5,592-7,456 miles) |

# JUNKERS

## Ju 187/Ju 287 (I)

The Junkers Ju 87 dive bomber, better known as the Stuka, was possibly the best known WWII aircraft, symbolic of the conflict. Its characteristic shape with the kinked wing is known not only to every enthusiast of aviation, but also to people with no such interest. It was the Ju 87 that started the war in September 1939. At the time the machines were at the peak of their capabilities. During the Battle of France they started to show their obsolescence, and the Battle of Britain ended their career in the West. Then virtually all Stukas were sent to the East, facing (initially) much weaker opponents.

Symptoms of obsolescence of the Stuka were noted fairly early on, and while it was still successful, work commenced on its successor. According to common practice, designations of such aircraft often repeated the last digits of the predecessor, such as the Ju 88 followed by the Ju 188, Ju 288 etc. Additionally, it has to be remembered that the RLM assigned batches of numbers to companies, to be allocated to individual designs. Thus, it is no wonder that the successor of the Ju 87 was going to be called the Ju 187, although the project was also known as the Ju 87F. In fact this project incorporated relatively few changes, and the idea was soon abandoned in favour of the more extensively redesigned Ju 287.

This first Ju 287 was going to be powered by the Jumo 213 in-line engine rated at 1,176 hp for take-off. Defensive armament was mounted in a remotelycontrolled turret, and included two 20mm MG 151/20 cannon. In addition, fixed forward-firing cannon were fitted in the wings. The cockpit was heavily armoured and the undercarriage was retractable. Air brakes were repositioned rearwards, onto the flaps, and the wing lost its characteristic inverted gullwing form and was straight in head-on view. The vertical tail had a very interesting design. The single fin and rudder could be rotated with the rear fuselage by 180° around the longitudinal axis, to a position below the fuselage, giving the gunner a free field of fire. It is worth noting that a similar idea was tested in Poland before the war on R-XIII aircraft, with a tail that could be lowered.

Design work reached the stage of an advanced mock-up and wind-tunnel models when the RLM lost its faith in the idea of a specialised dive bomber. In any case, the new aircraft was not much better than the Ju 87. In October 1943, this scepticism was so strong that the Ju 187/287 Stuka programme was eventually abandoned. The company was left with no more than a wooden mock-up and an unallocated type number 287.

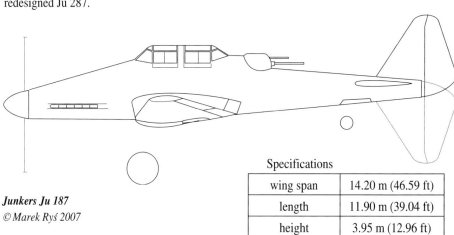

**Junkers Ju 187**
© Marek Ryś 2007

| Specifications | |
|---|---|
| wing span | 14.20 m (46.59 ft) |
| length | 11.90 m (39.04 ft) |
| height | 3.95 m (12.96 ft) |

# EF.100

Junkers joined the club of strategic bomber makers by preparing the EF.100 project, a passenger aircraft with a range of 9,000km. It was developed from 1940 for Deutsche Lufthansa, and then the RLM requested its conversion into a bomber with a useful load of 5,000kg. The aircraft had a very interesting design with a very broad fuselage, which to some extent played the role of another lift-generating surface. Power was going to be provided by six 2,500 hp Jumo 223 24-cylinder piston engines. The tricycle undercarriage retracted into the fuselage and engine nacelles. Several wind-tunnel models were built and tested.

In 1941 Junkers halted work on the EF.100. The RLM attempted to revive it as a long-range maritime reconnaissance aircraft, but eventually in 1942 the Ministry abandoned it completely.

Specifications:

| wing span | 65.00 m (213.25 ft) |
|---|---|
| length | 49.80 m (163.38 ft) |
| height | 9.00 m (29.52 ft) |
| wing area | 350.00 m² (3,767.49 sq ft) |
| empty weight | 44,000 kg (97,003 lb) |
| max. take-off weight | 81,000 kg (178,575 lb) |
| top speed | 550 km/h (342 mph) |
| ceiling | N/A |
| range | 9,000 km (5592 miles) |

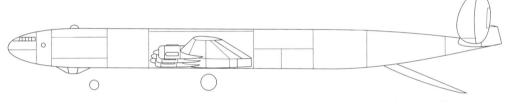

*Junkers EF-100*
*© Marek Ryś 2007*

# EF.116 (EF.57)

In 1943 a team of designers under Prof. Ing. Heinrich Hertel and Ing. Hans Wock commenced work on a bomber designated the EF.116, which would be able to carry 4,000kg of bombs. The aircraft had a conventional fuselage and tail, but very unusual wings. These were swept back by 25° in the inboard sections and swept forward by 23.5° in the outer sections. This was similar to that proposed for the Blohm und Voss P.188 bomber. The EF.116 was going to be powered by four Jumo 004H engines located in pairs under the wings.

Wind tunnel tests were undertaken in 1943: their results were very promising and ensured better flying characteristics than aircraft with a simple swept wing. Nevertheless, after the tests were completed the entire programme was cancelled.

Specifications:

| wing span | 26.50 m (86.94 ft) |
|---|---|
| length | 22.10 m (72.50 ft) |
| height | N/A |
| wing area | N/A |
| empty weight | N/A |
| max. take-off weight | N/A |
| top speed | 980 km/h (609 mph) |
| ceiling | N/A |
| range | 5,500 km (3418 miles) |

# EF.130

At the beginning of 1943, Junkers, in cooperation with DFS, started work on a long range bomber with a flying wing layout. Because this was a co-operative project, the aircraft is known in the literature both as the EF.130 and the DFS 130.

The aircraft had a mixed construction: the fuselage and central wing section was made of metal, and the outer wing sections were wood. The forward section of the aircraft housed a pressurised cockpit for the crew of three, the cockpit smoothly blending into the wing. Two fins were located at the trailing edge. The wing centre section housed the bomb bay and main wheel wells. The nose wheel unit retracted into the 'fuselage' under the cockpit. Remotely-controlled turrets were to be located on the upper surface of the wings. An internal bomb bay would accommodate up to 4,000kg of bombs. The EF.130 would be powered by four 9.8 kN BMW 003C jet engines located side-by-side above the wing.

The EF.130 programme had a rather low priority and did not proceed beyond the aerodynamic model stage.

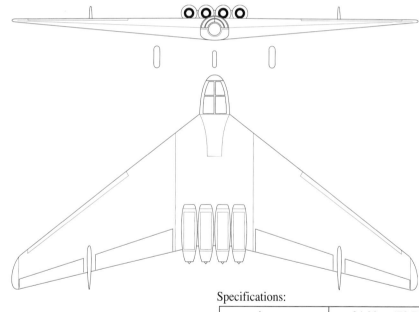

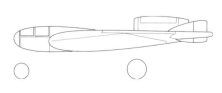

***Junkers EF.130***
*© Marek Ryś 2007*

Specifications:

| | |
|---|---|
| wing span | 24.00 m (78.74 ft) |
| length | 9.10 m (29.85 ft) |
| height | N/A |
| wing area | 120.00 m² (1291.71 sq ft) |
| empty weight | N/A |
| max. take-off weight | 38,100 kg (83,996 lb) |
| top speed | 950 km/h (590 mph) |
| ceiling | 6,000-11,500 m (19,685-37,730 ft) |
| range | 7,500 km (4,660 miles ) |

# EF.132

This heavy, six-engined bomber was one of the last projects from Junkers. Its beginnings can be traced back to 1942 when study work on a future jet bomber for the Luftwaffe commenced.

The studies produced a series of projects, which led to the Ju 287, the jet bomber with forward swept wings, known also under the company designation of EF.131. The innovative aerodynamic concept would likely have caused problems in service with the production machines that were proposed. To avoid this, a more conventional layout bomber, the EF.132, was developed as a backup design.

The EF.132 was a completely independent design, although it shared some features with the EF.131, such as the cockpit which housed five crew members under extensive glazing. This cockpit was located at the forward end of the fuselage and was a sort of Junkers 'trademark'. Aft of the cockpit, the fuselage housed the forward wheel well (under the cockpit), a three-section bomb bay, and fuel tanks. The wings were tapered, swept at 37° and had a slight anhedral of a few degrees. The outer sections would probably house fuel tanks and the main wheel wells. The inboard wing sections housed engine bays. The horizontal tail was dihedral and swept. The fin was mounted at the rear of the fuselage.

The aircraft was going to be defended by its six 20mm MG 151/20 cannon, which were mounted in pairs in three remotely-controlled turrets. The first of these turrets was located aft of the cockpit, the second under the fuselage, and the third at the rear. The 12m long bomb bay could accommodate 4,000-5,000 kg of bombs.

As regards the undercarriage, surviving documents and other sources mention twin nose wheels, twin main wheels under the rear fuselage (in tandem) and additional stabilising wheels under the outer wing sections. But drawings suggest a classic tricycle undercarriage with nose wheels, and main wheels retracting into the wings.

The aircraft was going to be powered by six 25 kN Junkers Jumo 012 jet engines. The engines were still under development, and they were to be mounted in an unusual way. Although the common practice was to fit engines in nacelles under the wings, in this design they were located inside the wing roots, thus minimising the aerodynamic drag.

At the beginning of 1945, a model of the aircraft was tested in a wind-tunnel. According to some sources a full scale wooden mock-up was built. However, the war ended at this point and Dessau was occupied by the Red Army, which captured all of the documentation left at the factory, the prototype Ju 287 V2, and the complete design team. It was the people and their knowledge that constituted the greatest value and they were to be used accordingly, working in the Soviet Union within the OKB-1 on both new and existing projects.

The decision to build the prototype of the EF.132 was taken at the end of 1945, and it was included in the work schedule for 1946. In October 1946 drawings were ready and, according to Soviet sources, the mock-up of the bomber was commenced. In theory there was no need to change the power plant, as the documentation of the Jumo 012 engine was also in Soviet hands. However, in 1946 the programme was cancelled and the prototype EF.132 was never built. Soviet sources suggest that the bomber was designed from scratch under Soviet control, but this is untrue. A lot of its features can be found in subsequent designs by Myasishchev and Tupolev.

*Junkers EF.132*
© *Marek Ryś 2007*

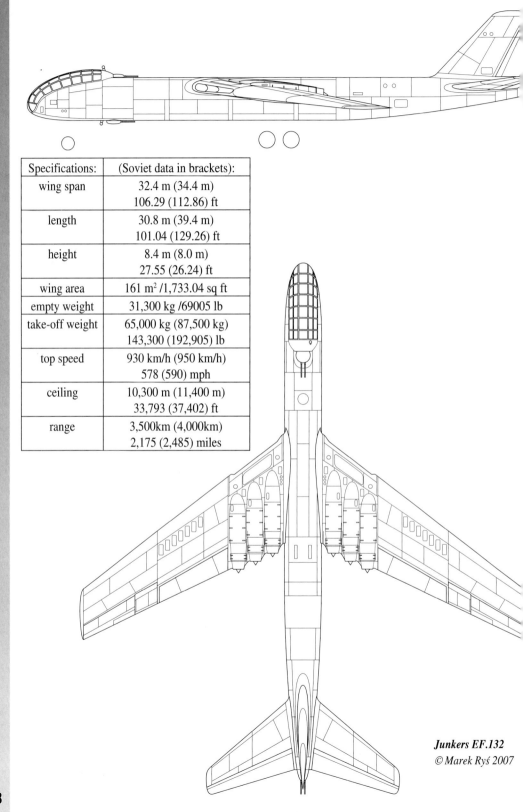

| Specifications: | (Soviet data in brackets): |
|---|---|
| wing span | 32.4 m (34.4 m) 106.29 (112.86) ft |
| length | 30.8 m (39.4 m) 101.04 (129.26) ft |
| height | 8.4 m (8.0 m) 27.55 (26.24) ft |
| wing area | 161 m² /1,733.04 sq ft |
| empty weight | 31,300 kg /69005 lb |
| take-off weight | 65,000 kg (87,500 kg) 143,300 (192,905) lb |
| top speed | 930 km/h (950 km/h) 578 (590) mph |
| ceiling | 10,300 m (11,400 m) 33,793 (37,402) ft |
| range | 3,500km (4,000km) 2,175 (2,485) miles |

*Junkers EF.132*

*© Marek Ryś 2007*

# JU 488

The Ju 488 illustrates very well that even such a serious task as the construction of a strategic bomber can be simplified by using available sub-assemblies from other aircraft, thereby reducing costs and making production easier.

In September of 1943 the RLM ordered Junkers at Dessau to develop a bomber possessing long range and good flying characteristics at high altitudes. The designers achieved this quite quickly by using the crew compartment and pressurised cockpit of the Ju 188T (Ju 388), the rear fuselage of the Ju 188E, the under-fuselage 'bathtub' and outer wing sections of the Ju 388K, and the twin tails of the Ju 288C. In addition, many other components – including engines – came from the Ju 88-288-388 family. Only the wing centre section and central fuselage were new. The aircraft was all-metal (except for the wooden under-fuselage pod) and a three-seat low-wing monoplane. It was powered by four BMW 801 TJ 14-cylinder, air cooled two-row radials rated at 1,800 hp for take-off and a maximum output of 1,890 hp at an altitude of 3,000 m. The undercarriage consisted of four main wheels which retracted into the engine nacelles, and a tail wheel. The first two prototypes were planned without any defensive armament. The fuselage housed a bomb bay for 5000kg of bombs.

Ju 488 V401 and V402 prototypes (the first and second prototypes) were built in France, in the former Latécoère factory at Toulouse. Inboard wing sections and the tail were assembled at Junkers factories in Bernburg and Dessau, and ferried to Toulouse for final assembly. In July of 1944, facing the rapid advance of Allied troops towards Toulouse, it was decided to ship the V401 and V402 airframes, at an advanced stage of completion, by rail to Bernburg. During the night of 16 July 1944, a group of resistance fighters under M. Elissalde, a fitter from Latécočre factory, seriously damaged the V401, preventing its transport. When the Germans evacuated the city in August of 1944, the fuselage of the V402 was found abandoned on a siding. It is not known what happened to the other components of the aircraft.

Construction of four more prototypes, V403-V406, was planned. These would differ significantly from their predecessors: they would have an entirely new fuselage and four 2,500 hp Jumo 222A/B-3 24-cylinder liquid cooled in-line engines. Their defensive armament consisted of two 20mm MG 151/20 cannon in a remotely-controlled turret on top of the rear fuselage and two 13mm MG 131 machine guns in a remotely-controlled tail position.

In November 1944 the RLM cancelled the order and no Ju 488 was ever completed.

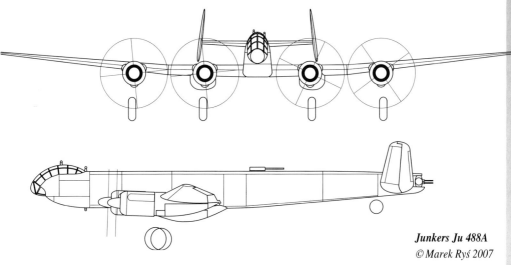

*Junkers Ju 488A*
*© Marek Ryś 2007*

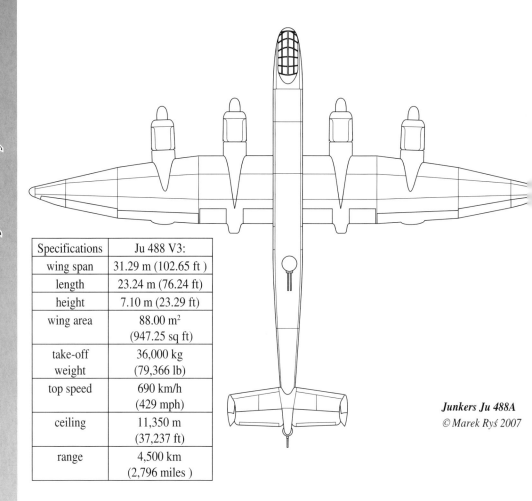

| Specifications | Ju 488 V3: |
|---|---|
| wing span | 31.29 m (102.65 ft ) |
| length | 23.24 m (76.24 ft) |
| height | 7.10 m (23.29 ft) |
| wing area | 88.00 m² (947.25 sq ft) |
| take-off weight | 36,000 kg (79,366 lb) |
| top speed | 690 km/h (429 mph) |
| ceiling | 11,350 m (37,237 ft) |
| range | 4,500 km (2,796 miles ) |

*Junkers Ju 488A*
© *Marek Ryś 2007*

# JU 290Z

Another way of obtaining a long-range bomber without incurring excessive cost, was to convert an existing design. Junkers tried this method both with the Ju 488 and the Ju 290 modification known as the Ju 290Z.

The Ju 290Z was going to be a pair of standard Ju 290As connected by a common wing centre section. The fuselages and tails were unaltered. Without a doubt, this was inspired by the success of a similar idea in the Heinkel He 111Z. Two fuselages and the additional space inside the new wing centre section allowed an increase in useful load and fuel tankage, the latter increasing the range of the machine which could reach up to 11,000km.

The aircraft was powered by eight BMW 801D engines.

The Ju 290Z was designed to be used both as a transport machine and as a bomber, and also as a carrier of rocket missiles for an attack on the USA. Its development was terminated in favour of the six-engined Ju 390.

Specifications:

| wing span | 60m (196.85 ft) |
|---|---|
| length | 28.00m (91.86 ft) |
| height | 6.90m (22.63 ft) |
| wing area | 88m² (947.25 sq ft) |
| take-off weight | 90,000kg (198,416 lb) |

# Ju 390

In the unofficial race for the 'Amerika Bomber', that is, a bomber able to attack American territory, pole position was occupied by the Ju 390. This was largely due to the fact that it was essentially a conversion of the series-produced Ju 290A, with a stretched fuselage and increased wingspan, and powered by six 1,970 hp BMW 801E engines. The aircraft was going to have a range of up to 12,000km. The Ju 390 could refuel in-flight, and could also serve as an in-flight tanker.

Work on the aircraft continued at the Prague department of Junkers, under Ing. Heinz Kraft. The size of the bomber was increased in a very simple manner by inserting additional segments in the fuselage and wings.

Three prototypes were ordered, of which only the first (GH+UK) and the second (RC+DA) were built. The third prototype was going to be the pattern example for the bomber version, armed with eight 20mm MG 151/20 cannon and four 13mm MG 131 machine guns, and carrying 1,800kg of bombs. It was never completed. The Ju 390 V2 was assigned to the Fernaufklärungs-Gruppe 5 at Mont de Marson in January 1944. It flew 32-hour patrol sorties, and during one of these the aircraft apparently came within 20km of the US coast, and returned to base.

| Specifications: | Ju 390 V1 |
|---|---|
| wing span | 50.32m (165.09 ft) |
| length | 33.40m (109.58 ft) |
| height | 6.10m (20.01 ft) |
| wing area | 254.30m² (2,737.35 ft) |
| empty weight | 35,910kg (79,168 lb) |
| take-off weight | 75,500kg (166,449 lb) |
| top speed | 473km/h (294 mph) |
| ceiling | 8,900m (29,200 ft) |
| range | 6,000-12,000km (3,728-7,456 miles) |

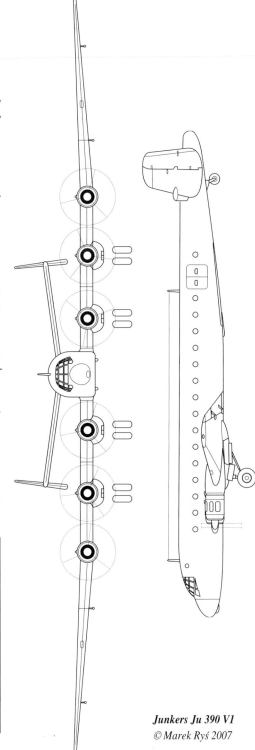

*Junkers Ju 390 V1*
© *Marek Ryś 2007*

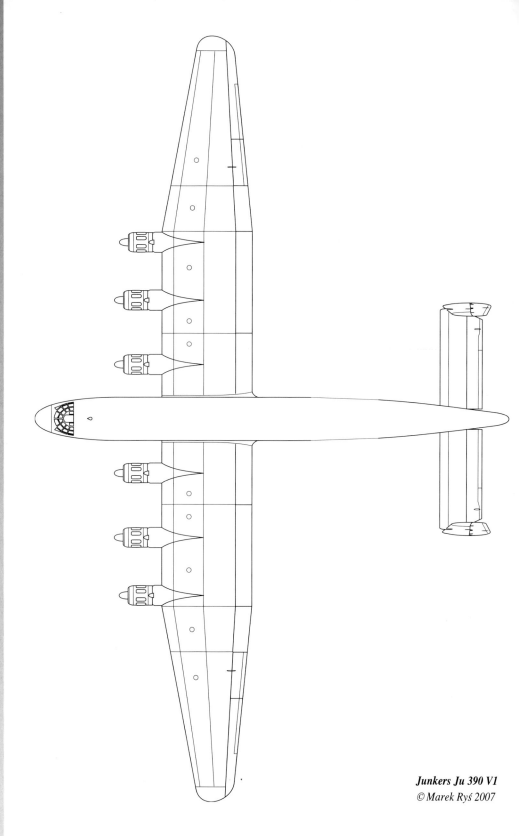

*Junkers Ju 390 V1*
© *Marek Ryś 2007*

# 287 (EF.122, EF.125, EF.131)

It is worth devoting more space to the Ju 287. This aircraft was the German dedicated jet bomber project that came closest to realisation, and it had a post-war continuation, influencing to some degree post-war aircraft technology in the Soviet Union.

The first proposals to sweep wings forward were suggested (in Germany) in about 1942. Ing. Philipp von Doepp from Junkers investigated the aerodynamic properties of the forward swept wing layout, and his research suggested that this arrangement could significantly improve flying characteristics compared to the swept back wing, which itself was innovative at the time. This was especially true with regards to ailerons efficacy, because they were set outside the zone of largest airflow vortices.

Von Doepp prepared a whole series of models that were subsequently tested in a wind-tunnel. It was then that he discovered another, adverse feature of the forward sweep: the need for high wing flexibility and strength. The wing tips, deflected upwards by the air stream, caused significant turning moments along the entire span of the wing. At the same time, this phenomenon allowed for higher angles of attack in flight. Because the designers needed to to maintain sufficient strength and flexibility of the wing, it could be used in no way other than the principal task, which was to generate lift. Fuel tanks and undercarriage wells had to be incorporated into the fuselage, as any disturbance of the internal structure (such as cut-outs in the spars for the retracted undercarriage) would dramatically weaken the wing. Also, fuel tanks inside the stressed aero-elastic wing structure would be prone to cracking. Components of the control and high-lift devices (ailerons, flaps, and possibly slats) had to be designed carefully, to prevent jamming.

Doepp's finding were useful to his parent company when the RLM placed an order for the development of a large jet powered bomber. The task was entrusted to the team under Prof. Heinrich Hertel, with Ing. Hans Wocke as the leading designer. Preliminary work had started already, in 1942. The preliminary designs showed a four-engined project,

at the time proposed with a 'normal' swept-back wing, with the sweep angle 25°.

A whole range of small wooden models was built and wind-tunnel tested, and various arrangements of individual components were tried, in order to check their effect on the airframe's chareteristics and performance. It was anticipated that the aircraft would reach speeds of the order of 0.8 Mach, and the wing would be designed for such speeds. However, while the problem of engine nacelle drag, or the behaviour of the whole airframe could be tested and refined in the wind tunnel, there were new problems that proved difficult to cure. It turned out that at low speeds, the wing tips vibrated, which would interfere with the aileron operation and affect the flight stability of the aircraft. Problems with these vibrations were subsequently eliminated using solutions such as additional aerodynamic fences to 'straighten' the air flow over the wing, or through altering the design of the wing airfoil.

It is worth remembering that at the time when Hertel's team were working on their bomber, the swept wing was still an avant-garde and unproven solution. Designers were forced to look for their own solutions, and did not have the experience of other teams to draw upon. A series of wind-tunnel tests in different configurations provided the conclusion that a reverse sweep may be a good method of controlling the vibration in the wing tips. This conclusion was based in part on experiments carried out earlier at the Deutsche Versuchsanstalt für Lufthart (DVL) using forward swept wings.

Today, it is difficult to say which member of the design team thought of the idea to turn the wing 'back to front' in the new bomber, but the final decision was eventually taken by Prof. Hertel, who was in charge of the project. More wind-tunnel models were built, and their tests proved that the idea of forward-swept wings was sound. The wing tips no longer vibrated, although the problem with upward bending did appear. However, this phenomenon was constant (and not variable, like the vibrations), and it was relatively easy to control.

Because of the forward-swept wings, significant improvements were achieved in the air flow around the wing, and the corresponding increase in the lifting force was especially important for a heavy bomber. The new layout had so many advantages that at this point attempts to cure the 'classic' swept wings were dropped and all work focused on the forward-swept wing.

At the time the available jet engines provided only relatively small amounts of thrust. It was enough to lift and accelerate a small fighter, but in the case of a bomber -- a heavier and larger aircraft -- it was necessary to fit more engines. At the same time, the designers realised that the wings could not be loaded too heavily, because at high speeds they were subject to significant G-loads. Wind-tunnel test carried out on subsequent models focused on identifying the optimum location of the power plants.

First of all, the design team realised that the minimum number of engines to lift the aircraft with the bomb load, fuel and crew, was four -- but six was preferable. However, because the bomber was going to be a relatively small aircraft, there were limited options for the location of the engines. One obvious idea was to fit them under the wings, and this type of model with four separate nacelles was tested, but it was soon abandoned for reasons to do with structural strength. Projects designated EF.58, EF.59, and EF.66 (an interesting project with the engines located on pylons at sides of the fuselage, that allowed adjustment of their position) were developed and built in model form for wind-tunnel tests.

The layout chosen eventually included two engines in nacelles over the wings and the other two on the sides of the forward fuselage. Soon the idea was modified, with the wing engines relocated under the wings. This led to the configuration that gave best results during testing. It was approved as the chosen solution, and the design team commenced more detailed study work, which resulted in the EF.122 project. Originally, this was going to be an all-metal mid-wing monoplane, powered by four Junkers Jumo 004 jet engines arranged according to the approved concept. The front of the fuselage housed a cockpit for the crew, with extensive glazing similar to the one used in the Ju 388, although not identical. The tricycle undercarriage, as planned from the very beginning, would

be retractable. The nose wheel would be retract into the fuselage and the main wheel units would retract partly into the fuselage (the wheels) and partly into the wings (the legs). The classic tail was going to consist of a fin and rudder, plus a tailplane with elevators. As for the elevators, it was not decided whether they should be straight or swept. Several models of the rear fuselage of the EF.122 were prepared, and these included, in addition to the tail, the FHL 151Z remotely-controlled turret at the rear of the fuselage, operated by a crew member using a persicopic sight. The turret was planned as standard equipment of the EF.122 and it was going to have two 20mm MG 151/20 cannon. Bombs would be carried in the fuselage bomb bay.

The preliminary project was sent to the RLM at the beginning of 1944. In March of that year, the Ministry ordered the company to build a prototype as quickly as possible, and allocated the designation Ju 287 again. It soon transpired that construction of the EF.122/Ju 287 in its final planned form was not realistic. First of all, the characteristics of the forward-swept wings were known solely from wind-tunnel tests and not from trials of any aircraft or gliders. Investing funds in construction of a bomber that could prove a complete failure due to its unorthodox configuration was too risky, and the Junkers company decided to build an experimental aircraft first, to investigate the innovative layout. To maximise the speed of its construction, they used components from other aircraft. The project was headed by Ing. Ernst Zindel.

The new aircraft, although it was only going to be a new technology testbed, received the designation Ju 287 V1. It was to be a hybrid of the He 177A-3 bomber fuselage (selected because its dimensions were similar to those of the planned Ju 287), with a modified rear section, the tail section of the Ju 388L-1, and completely new, tapered, forward-swept wings (with a sweep of 25°). To maintain structural strength in the wings and to avoid unnecessary modifications to the airframe, the designers decided to use a fixed undercarriage. The undercarriage parts also came from other aircraft: the main wheels were taken from the Ju 352A-1, while the twin nose wheels came from downed B-24 Liberators. All of the wheels were covered by large spats. The aircraft was powered by four

8.9 kN (900 kG) Junkers Jumo 004B-2 jet engines. Two of these were located in nacelles under the wings, and two on the sides of the forward fuselage near the cockpit. Fuel tanks were located in the fuselage, where measurement equipment was also housed. The crew was just two men: the pilot and the flight engineer/radio operator. The aircraft was built as a mid-wing monoplane, and because the Ju 287 V1 no armament was included.

On 16 August, 1944 the prototype, bearing the call-sign RS+RA and with the Junkers chief company test pilot Flugkapitän Siegfried Holzbauer at the controls, took off for the first time. Evidently, the designers underestimated the performance of the machine, as it lifted off after a run of only one-third the length of the runway! Additional rocket boosters proved unnecessary.

Another 17 flights took place without major problems. Meanwhile, a pitot tube was added on the starboard wing, the airframe was covered with cotton tufts in the crucial areas, and a cine camera was fitted above the rear fuselage on a special mount forward of the tail, to film the behaviour of the tufts in flight. The nose wheel spats were soon abandoned, and the aircraft was used for low speed trials. This was understandable, as the maximum speed of the Ju 287 V1 was 650 km/h.

The first information about the new aircraft reached the Allies at the beginning of 1945, when the prototype was moved to the Erprobungsstelle (Testing center) at Rechlin. A high flying reconnaissance Mosquito photographed it on the runway. Photographic interpreters spotted an unusual shape in one of the frames, and labelled it 'Rechlin 66'. (This followed the standard naming system for unknown German designs found by aerial reconnaissance or by other means. The designation included the name of the place of first identification (Rechlin in this case) and the estimated span of the 'unidentified object' in feet (in this case it was estimated very accurately at 66 feet or 20.1 m).) Soon afterwards, Rechlin was thoroughly pounded with Allied bombs which, apart from general destruction, seriously damaged the prototype Ju 287 V1. It was soon repaired, and camouflaged in a wood on the outskirts of the aerodrome, where it stayed until April 1945, when it was captured by the Soviets.

While the Ju 287 V1 was making its first flights, the design team continued to be hard at

Specifications:

| Version | Ju 287 V1 | Ju 287 V3 | EF-131 | 140 | 140-R | 140-B/R |
|---|---|---|---|---|---|---|
| wing span (m) (ft) | 20.11 (65.98) | 19.40 (63.65) | 19.40 (63.65) | 19.40 (63.65) | 21.90 (71.85) | 21.90 (71.85) |
| length (m) (ft) | 18.30 (60.04) | 19.767 (64.852) | 20.47 (67.16) | 19.50 (63.98) | 19.50 (63.98) | 19.50 (63.98) |
| height (m) (ft) | 5.10 (16.73) | 5.7 (18.70) | 5.7 (18.70) | 5.7 (18.70) | 5.7 (18.70) | 5.7 (18.70) |
| wing area (m²) (sq ft) | 58.30 (627.54) | 58.00 (624.31) | 58.00 (624.31) | 58.00 (624.31) | 61.00 (656.60) | 61.00 (656.60) |
| empty (kg) (lb) | 12,510 (27,580) | 11,930 (26,301) | N/A | N/A | N/A | N/A |
| take-off (kg) (lb) | 20,000 (44,092) | 21,555 (47,521) | 22,955 (50,607) | 23,000 (50,706) | 25,540 (56,306) | 26,100 (57,540) |
| top speed (km/h) (mph) | 559 (347) | 860 (534) | 860 (534) | 904 (562) | 837 (520) | 866 (538) |
| cruising speed (km/h) (mph) | 512 (318) | 792 (492) | N/A | N/A | N/A | N/A |
| ceiling (m) (ft) | 10,800 (35,433) | 10,620 (34,842) | 12,500 (41,000) | 11,700 (38,400) | 14,100 (15,400) | 13,600 (14,900) |
| range (km) (miles) | 1,500 (932) | 4,416* (2,744) | 1,710 (1,063) | 2,000 (1,243) | 3,600 (2,237) | 2,700 (1,678) |

* — maximum range without bomb load; the range was 1,900 km with 3,000 kg of bombs, and 2,120 km with 2,000 kg.

work, preparing the design of the actual bomber. This included analysis of the aircraft propulsion. As mentioned before, both a four engine and a six engine layout were considered. These proposed layouts used BMW 003A-1 engines, which had a thrust of 7.85 kN (800kg); slightly lower than that of the Jumo 004. Two basic arrangements were considered. The first clustered four engines in two nacelles under the wings and left the other two on the sides of the forward part of the fuselage. The other concept mounted all six engines under the wings, in clusters of three. Both of these configurations were going to be tested in subsequent prototypes. In addition, wind-tunnel models of the EF.122 were also tested with various arrangements of the engines under the wings: in an attempt to find the optimum solution, the engines were shifted fore and aft. A series of intriguing and mysterious photos survive from that period of tests, which depict models of some project versions about which we know very little. Other photos show a model of an EF.122 variant fitted with a new cockpit canopy with an unglazed front portion, the cockpit most probably housing electronic equipment.

If and when new engine types became available, serious changes to the design were going to be needed. With newer engines offering significantly higher thrust than the Jumo 004 or BMW 003, the total number of engines on the Ju287 could be reduced to just two, as in the EF.125 project. This significantly reduced the weight of the aircraft and its drag. However, none of these power plants actually became available before the end of the war.

The variant with six BMW 003A engines was selected as the first to be built. This project, designated the EF.131. The orignal plan for the Ju 287 V2 was not to use six engines, but to use four 9.8 kN (990 kG) Jumo 004C engines. These were not available for the foreseeable future, and so the six-engined version was built instead.

The aircraft had a new fuselage, with the extensively glazed cockpit (for the entire crew) located at the very front. The cockpit arrangement was based on the Ju 288 bomber. This gave the bomb-aimer/navigator, seated at the front, excellent visibility in all directions (except to the rear, of course). Behind the cockpit, the fuselage housed fuel tanks, the bomb bay and the main wheel wells.

The EF.131 was designed to have a FHL 151Z turret with two 15mm MG 151 cannon at the rear of the fuselage. It was remotely controlled via a periscopic sight by the gunner/radio operator, who sat behind the pilot, facing the rear of the aircraft. Eventually, it was decided that the Ju 287 V2 would not be fitted with the gun position. This decision was due to the haste with which the prototype was built. The FHL 151Z remotely-controlled position, that was also going to be used in the Ju 288, 388 and 488, was still undeveloped, and during ground tests and Ju 288 and 388 prototype test flights it posed a lot of problems. According to the design team, the Ju 287 jet was going to be fast enough to make defensive armament unnecessary. The designers therefore did not wish to include the guns, but RLM officials believed that an aircraft without any guns could not be suitable for combat use. In the case of the Ju 287, however, the idea to turn it into a 'flying fortress' was not pursued. This would not be feasible anyway, considering the performance of the jet engines available: the fully loaded aircraft weighed no less than 21,555kg, including 3,000kg of bombs carried in the fuselage bay, and the engines could not have handled the extra weight of the turret and gun position.

As regards the rest of the design; the tricycle undercarriage was retractable, with the nose wheel unit completely housed in a bay in the fuselage, and the main wheel units retracting in such a manner that the legs were stored in wing bays. The wheels rotated as the undercarriage retracted, so that they could be housed in the fuselage vertically.

The wing span of the Ju 287 V2 was slightly shorter than that of the Ju 287 V1, but geometrically it was identical. Apart from the forward-swept wings, the other most characteristic feature of the second prototype was its six 7.84 kN BMW 003A jet engines, mounted in a peculiar arrangement under the wings. They were set in two clusters of three engines, and a single engine was mounted lower and slightly forward of the upper two. This kind of arrangement gave the crew a bit more comfort than the earlier layout in which two engines were mounted on the sides of the cockpit. The lower engine positioned slightly forward of the other two reduced the adverse weight distribution and ensured better balance of the the aircraft's mass.

Assembly of the Ju 287 V2 commenced while trials of the first prototype were still underway, but it continued very slowly. A model was wind-tunnel tested, while a very exact wooden mock-up of the fuselage and cockpit was built in the workshops. Extensive photographic coverage of the mock-up survives, so we know exactly what the aircraft was going to look like. One cluster of three BMW 003A-1 engines was prepared for ground tests.

Work on the prototype continued at a very slow pace, and it slowed down even further when in July 1944 the RLM decided to stop all work on bombers in favour of fighters. Of course such a radical order could never be fully implemented. Work continued, in part unknown to the Ministry, at the company's own cost. This proved to be a far-sighted approach, as in March 1945 a new directive of the RLM ordered mass production of the Ju 287 to start as soon as possible. At the time, the prototype was at an advanced stage of assembly, but soon afterwards it fell in the hands of the Soviets, as did the V1.

Problems with the balance of the aircraft's mass with the six engines under the wings, as well as the trouble the design team had in ensuring sufficient stiffness of the wing (after all, the weight of six engines attached mid-span was not trivial) led to studies of different engine arrangements. The third prototype, Ju 287 V3, was going to have four BMW 003A-1 engines located in clusters of two under the wings and two more such engines mounted, as in the Ju 287 V1, on the sides of the forward fuselage.

Ju 287 V3 was going to be fully armed (with a FHL 151Z position in the tail) and would become a pattern example for the production of Ju 287A-1. One aircraft was going to be completed as the Ju 287A-0, identical to the V3. It was planned that series production would commence as soon as it was possible, and that by December 1945 it would reach the rate of 100 machines a month. Also, a full scale detailed mock-up was built for the Ju 287 V3, but work on the prototype did not even start.

It was a similar story with other planned aircraft. The Ju 287 V4, which was to be the pattern for the production Ju 287A-2, was going to be built by ATG (Allgemein Transportanlagen GmbH) at Merserburg near Leipzig, and would be powered by six 9.8 kN Junkers Jumo 004C engines in two clusters under the wings, or two under the wings and two on the sides

of the fuselage. The Ju 287 V5 would have four 12.5 kN Heinkel Hirth 011 engines under the wings and would be the prototype for the Ju 287B-1 version. The Ju 287 V6 (Ju 287B-2 in series production) was going to be powered by two 33 kN BMW 018 or 29.4 kN Junkers 012 engines. Both these machines would be fitted with ejection seats. Needless to say, none of these machines were built.

German documents mentioned designations EF.123, 124 and 129, but nothing is known about these. It is therefore not possible to say if these were in any way connected with the Ju 287 programme.

The Ju 287 had a stiff competitor in the form of the Heinkel He 343, a bomber of proven design, which, however, was rejected by RLM . In a situation in which jet propulsion itself was a complete novelty, still in testing, the choice of the He 434 made obvious sense. And yet the RLM decided to bet on the unorthodox Ju 287, showing only slight interest in the Heinkel design. This was probably not for technical reasons, but due to the well-known personal dislike of Heinkel on the part of some officials at the Ministry. On 25 May, 1944 a conference was held at Berchtesgaden, and this was officially confirmed

Supposedly, one of the last planned versions of the Ju 287 was an unmanned variant that would have formed the bottom, explosive part of the Mistel 4, in which a Me 262 was the director aircraft. The Ju 287 was going to be filled with explosives and it would take-off using a special trolley. Near the target the flying bomb would separate from the Me 262 and fly towards the target, radio-guided from the Me 262. Drawings of this sort of combination were published for many years in numerous publications describing the Me 262 Schwalbe (including one such publication by the author). However, it turns out that German documents include no trace of such an idea with regards to the Ju 287. The first information about this Mistel 4 combination was published in July 1949 in Interavia magazine, and this seems to be the oldest source that mentions the Me 262/Ju 287 Mistel 4. It can therefore be surmised that this combination might have been a post-war invention of the author of that first article, and not a plan belonging to the German engineers. (Unless the creators of 'The Fourth Reich', hidden in remote parts of the Alps or abroad, continued their design work and the results were published in magazines.)

May 1945 was the end of the '1000 Year Reich', but not the end of the Ju 287. The Soviet Union, fighting the victorious war against 'Hitler's reptile' had significantly better equipment and armament, better aircraft, better tanks, better ships -- and generally everything it had was better. Or at least that was what *Pravda* ('Truth') newspaper and 'informburo' announcements claimed. But the Soviets seized every opportunity to capture this 'inferior' German equipment and aircraft. Another myth, this one perpetuated by those who recalled the excesses of the 'liberating' Red Army, said that the Soviets demolished everything they could lay their hands on. It seems they did not.

When the Soviets entered German territory at the beginning of 1945, the National Defence Committee (GKO – Gosudarstvenniy komitet oborony) formed a department known as NKAP. This dealt with securing the remains of German aircraft technology in the captured German territories and in the 'liberated' countries, especially in Austria and Czechoslovakia. Factory tooling, military equipment, and technical devices were dismantled and shipped to the USSR, as part of the 'reparations' for the losses inflicted by the German invasion of 1941 and as compensation for the costs borne when reorganising the arms industry following its evacuation deep into Russia.

Apart from physical assets, the Red Army captured a much greater treasure: thousands of German engineers, technicians, and skilled workers. Their knowledge and experience had a colossal effect on the USSR's technology. Particular importance was attached to questions of radio technology and of jet and rocket propulsion, as the Soviets' own experience in this area was weak. A committee for jet technology was organised at the GKO,

and its main role, among others, was to use German experience in the design of jet engines, including both those series in production (the BMW 003 and Jumo 004), and those still on the drawing-board. The idea to use German staff for their subsequent development was put forward during the summer of 1945. On 27 June, A. I. Shakhurin, the Minister of Aircraft Industry, issued a letter to the CK VKP(b) (in which he suggested using German experts held by the NKVD (Narodny Komissariat Vnutrennikh Delfor work in the aircraft industry under Soviet control. The suggestion was accepted and the 'brain drain' commenced.

Among the many companies and aircraft plants of the Third Reich that were visited by the Soviets, the Junkers works at Dessau (with its staff) were without a doubt the crucial prize. It was there that the OTB-1 was formed, subsequently reformed into the OKB-1. At the same time the achievements of the NKAP regarding German aircraft technology were assessed. The paragraph in Order No 874-366ss dated on 17 April 1946, that is most interesting for us is the one that covers 'taking over the entire documentation of all jet aircraft developed by the Junkers company, both projects and the realised ones, including the E-126 attack and Ju 287 bomber aircraft'.

In 1946, the OKB-1, formed at Dessau, had approximately 500 people working in the parent factory alone. As of October 1946, it included a total of 4,247 people, including 32 Soviet engineers, 1,131 German engineers and 3,084 German workers. The chief designer was the former Junkers chief designer Dr. Brunolf Wilhelm Baade, and on the Soviet side the enterprise was supervised by Petr N. Obrubov, an engineer from 'factory no. 240'. The OKB had separate engine and aircraft departments. Tasks for the latter were detailed in the letter No. 874-366ss of 17 April 1946, issued

*Ju 287 V3/Ju 287A-1*
© *Marek Ryś 2007*

by the Soviet Council of Ministers. The office was directed to:

a). complete the construction of the Junkers-131 bomber prototype with six Jumo-004 engines (!), with a top speed of 860 km/h, bomb load of 2,000kg and range of 1,050km. Time of completion of construction – September 1946.

b). complete the technical project of the Junkers-132 long range jet bomber with six Jumo-012 engines, at a speed of 950 km/h, bomb load of 4,000kg and range of 2,250km. Time of completion of the project work – December 1946.

c). complete the construction of the Junkers-126 jet attack aircraft with Jumo-226 'Argus' engine (speed 780km/h) and carry out during May-June 1946 flying trials in USSR territory.'

(n.b. The specification of 'Jumo-226 'Argus' or six 'Jumo-004' under the wings of the 'Junkers-131' were used in the original document.)

The Ju 287 V2 was the greatest (and biggest) rarity found at Dessau. The aircraft was at an advanced stage of completion and was not damaged. Completing it was not a real problem, but it was decided not to assemble

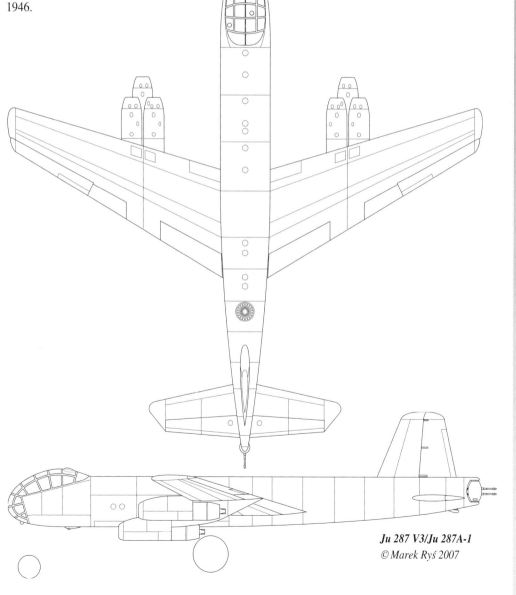

*Ju 287 V3/Ju 287A-1*
© *Marek Ryś 2007*

it in its original form, but to modify it slightly. F. Freitag and G. Bokke were appointed the designers responsible for preparing the project, while the work would be supervised by B. Baade.

It transpired that part of the documentation had to be prepared a new, and the unfinished aircraft was disassembled. The reworked EF-131 was slightly longer than its predecessor and the fuselage was assembled partly from ready Ju 287 V2 components, and partly from new ones. The wings and tail were left unchanged. Power was provided by six original German engines, mounted, as planned, in triple clusters under the wings. One problem is that according to Soviet materials these were Jumo 004B engines and not the BMW 003A-1 engines as planned by the Germans. It is difficult to be certain, as Soviet documents include many inaccuracies (such as the information about the He 219 with DB 610 engines), but it would seem logical to replace the planned power plants with more powerful ones, which were also available in larger numbers.

According to the plan, three EF-131 examples were going to be built: V1, V2 and V3. The first and the third prototypes were allocated for flight tests, while the second one was for strength testing. In May of 1946 wind-tunnel trials of an aerodynamic model commenced. Construction of a full-scale wooden mock-up was completed in June, and it was demonstrated to the VVS committee under Gen. Ushakov, and the committee decided that the EF-131 would be a valuable acquisition for the Soviet air force. It was postulated that the armament should be reinforced, while the ejection seat and emergency cockpit canopy jettison systems should be replaced.

On 12 August, 1946 the prototype was complete and ready for ground trials. The wings had a sweep of –19.5° at the leading edge, power was provided by six Jumo 004Bs, the armament in the FHL 151Z tail turret consisted of two 13mm machine guns (probably German MG 131s). The take-off weight was 22,955kg, and the fuel load 7,150kg. Seven 9.10 kN (1,000 kG) take-off booster rockets were to be used. On 16 August, EF-131 V1 was transferred for flying trials, but no take-off took place. In occupied Germany, construction or production of any aircraft was banned, not to mention the fact that any German pilot tasked with test flying

the prototype might land in the wrong occupation zone, and Soviet fighters might not be able to stop him. In September of 1946, the EF-131 V1 was disassembled and shipped to the USSR, where it was transferred to the LII (Lotno Issliedowatielnyj Institut – Aviation Institute). Soon afterwards, the whole staff of the OKB-1 went to the USSR.

Before the first flight the aircraft required a number of corrections to the design. The fuselage proved too weak to be likely to survive high speed flight, and limiting the speed to 600km/h did not make much sense. Modifications took about two months, and assembly of the second EF-131 prototype continued. Eventually, on 23 May 1947, the EF-131 V1 took off from Stakhanovism aerodrome (now Zhukovskiy) for its first flight, piloted by the German Paul Junge. Take-off was easy and the aircraft lifted off at 250km/h. The first flight was going to be purely for early tests and the speed did not exceed 350km/h. Having climbed to 1,400m, the machine made a short straight and level flight at a speed of 220km/h. During the landing run the port main wheel leg attachment failed and the undercarriage collapsed. Damage was not serious, however, and following the replacement of the engine and main wheel leg, flying continued.

In September 1947, the new Minister of Aircraft Industry sent a letter to S. L. Rebenko, the acting manager of the OKB-1, requesting that EF-131 V1 testing should be completed by the end of October and a report delivered to him on 1 November 1947. Had everything gone according to plan, the machine would have taken part in a flying parade on 7 November.

Failures plagued the prototype, however, and the programme of trials was not completed in time. The nose undercarriage failed, the tail vibrated… and the aircraft spent more time in the hands of the ground crew than in the air. By October 1947, only seven flights had been made, for a total flying time of 4.5 hours. The same month saw the introduction of strict limitations regarding the presence of foreign specialists in the Soviet secret test centres. This resulted in a virtual halt of the work on the EF-131 and EF-126, and the prototypes of these machines were left at the aerodrome, covered with snow. By the time the snow thawed in the spring, a good deal of damage had been done. Repairs continued for several months and it took until June 1948 before the preparation of the EF-131 V1 prototype for flying was completed. The prototype was transferred to Tepliy Stan aerodrome near Moscow, but before the first take-off took place, the Minister of Aircraft Industry issued order No. 440 of 21 June 1948 to stop further work on the aircraft.

In October of 1948, S. M. Alekseyev, who maintained friendly relations with B. Baade, was appointed the manager of the OKB-1. They continued work on the main task assigned to the design office: trials of the aircraft designated EF-140 in German terminology, or '140' in Soviet documents. In fact, this was a modification of the EF-131, powered by two Mikulin AM-TRDK-01 jet engines of Soviet design. Their thrust was much higher that that of the German Jumo 004 and reached approximately 32.4 kN (3,300kg), allowing for a reduction in the number of engines. The engines were located in single nacelles under the wings, and the prototype was built using components of the EF-131 V1 that were no longer used, including the tail and wings.

The armament was altered by replacing the FHL 151Z tail position with two remotely-controlled turrets on top of the fuselage (aft of the cockpit) and under the fuselage near the wing trailing edge. Each of these turrets was fitted with two 20mm cannon. The crew of the bomber rose from two to four. The pilot was seated at the front of the cockpit on the port side, with the bomb-aimer by his side. The dorsal turret gunner was seated behind the pilot, facing backwards, and by his side was the position of the gunner/radio operator, who operated the ventral turret. Both of the gunners had periscopic sights. The central fuselage housed the bomb bay for 4,500kg of bombs.

Work on the project was commenced in 1947 by B. Baade under his own initiative. During the following year, a mock-up was completed and approved by a committee, and by September 1948, the prototype was built. After the aircraft was assembled, the first take-off took place on 30 September from Tepliy Stan, and it lasted 20 minutes. Subsequent flights revealed serious instability in the engines, which could not provide continuous thrust: the amount of thrust fluctuated unpredicatbly, which made flying difficult. After the seventh flight, the aircraft was grounded. In 1949 the engines were

replaced and on 24 May factory tests were resumed and a top speed of 904km/h and range of 2,000km were theoretically achievable.

No state trials of the prototype were carried out, probably because the Tu-14 was selected for production instead. It had been clear even some time before, that the '140' had little chance of entering service with the VVS as a bomber -- and this is why, in May of 1948, its reconnaissance variant '140-R' was already being developed. This '140-R' differed in equipment, had wings with significantly longer span, with additional fuel tanks at the tips and with 26.5 kN (2,700kg) Klimov VK-1 engines. The engines were in fact modified Rolls Royce Nene 1s manufactured in the USSR. With the new power source and larger wing area, the potential range of the aircraft rose to 3,600km and the ceiling to 14,100m. The defensive armament was left virtually unchanged, except that the 20mm cannon were replaced with 23mm cannons. Both turrets were coupled with the aiming system, so that they could both be controlled by one gunner. Photographic equipment was fitted in the bomb bay and in the rear fuselage. As the Germans no longer had access to the VVS base of Tepliy Stan near the factory, a factory airfield was arranged at Borki village, and on 12 October ,1949, I. E. Fedotov first flew the '140-R'. Both the first and subsequent flights ended in emergency landings due to wing vibration, and the aircraft went back to the workshop, where it was discovered that the vibrations were due to the fuel tanks at the wing tips.

In August of 1948, Baade was tasked with developing another version, designated '140-B/R'. This was going to combine the bomber and reconnaissance roles. It differed from its predecessor in having a slightly shorter wing span and different equipment. The prototype was built and it passed ground testing, but the problems that had plagued the '140-R' persisted. Eventually, on 18 July 1950, work on the aircraft was halted by orders from above, and the forward-swept wing was abandoned in the USSR, as it failed to offer significantly better characteristics than the normal swept wing. Work on such layout was terminated completely in 1952. It was revived on 25 September 1998, when the Sukhoi S-37 took off -- but that is another story...!

# VERY LONG RANGE BOMBER 1945

Several weeks before the end of the war, RLM officials received documentation about a long range bomber project developed by Junkers in cooperation with DFS. This long range bomber was a flying wing machine without any fuselage and with a single fin. The aircraft had all-metal construction and a tricycle undercarriage, and it was powered by four HeS 011A or Jumo 012 engines located completely inside the wings, side-by-side in pairs of two. Because the main undercarraige was a narrow track type, stabilising outriggers were added, which retracted into the wings. The bomb bay was located on both sides of the wing centre section.

This bomber was intended to be able to carry 8,000 kg of bombs over a distance of 17,000km!

Specifications:

| | |
|---|---|
| wing span | 51.30 m (168.30 ft ) |
| length | 31.00 m (101.70 ft) |
| height | N/A |
| wing area | 1,100.00 m² (11,841 sq ft) |
| empty weight | N/A |
| take-off weight | 90,000 kg (198,416 lb) |
| top speed | 1,030 km/h (640 mph) |
| ceiling | N/A |
| range | 17,000 km (10,563 miles) |

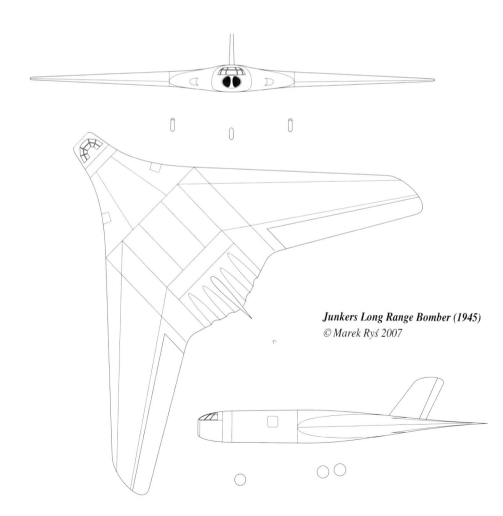

***Junkers Long Range Bomber (1945)***
*© Marek Ryś 2007*

# LIPPISCH

## P.10-108 (May 1942)

The designations of aircraft projects from Alexander Lippisch's office suffer from numerous misunderstandings and erroneous interpretations. This confusion is due to different designs having the same designation in documents. Lippisch did not have a permanent base in the form of a factory, plant, or workshop, and was a independent contractor to the Messerschmitt company. It was therefore a reasonable assumption that his projects would be developed by them.

The P.10-108, of May 1942, was a fast bomber which had little in common with the P.10 of November 1941, the latter being an attack aircraft. Ing. Wurster and Ing. Hubert were the leading designers on the P.10-108 project. The aircraft had a tailless layout with swept wings, and was going to be of mixed construction. Its design strongly resembled the Me 163 Komet which had also been designed by Lippisch.

The P.10-108 aircraft was a single-seat low-wing monoplane. It had a retractable tail wheel undercarriage. The cockpit was covered by a tear-drop canopy, and it featured small windows in the nose, to facilitate the pilot's view during take-off and landing. Power was provided by the 2,400 hp DB 606 24-cylinder in-line engine (two coupled DB 601s), driving a four metre four-bladed pusher propeller. The armament was going to consist of two MG 151/20 cannon in the forward fuselage and two 30mm MK 108 cannon in the rear. The fuselage bomb bay housed 1,000kg of bombs.

Because of the relationship between Lippisch and Messerschmitt the aircraft was apparently designated in some documents as the Me 334.

Specifications:

| | |
|---|---|
| wing span | 18.00m (59.05 ft) |
| length | 9.85m (32.31 ft) |
| height | 6.00 m (19.68 ft) |
| wing area | 53.00m$^2$ (570.50 sq ft) |
| empty weight | N/A |
| take-off weight | 11,000kg (24,250 lb) |
| top speed | N/A |
| ceiling | N/A |
| range | N/A |

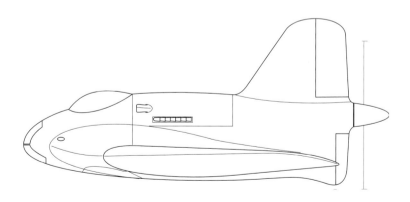

*Lippisch P.10-108*
*© Marek Ryś 2007*

# P.11-92

Another Schnellbomber project from Lippisch, the twin-jet P.11-92, was developed after September 1942 under the direction of Ing. Hendrick. This aircraft took their favoured tailless layout, and it had swept wings with a leading edge sweep of 30°. The crew of two was seated back-to-back in the pressurised cockpit under a common teardrop shaped canopy. The tricycle undercarriage retracted into the fuselage and wings.

The aircraft was powered by two Jumo 004C engines, and Rheinmetall-Borsig solid fuel rocket boosters, located in the fuselage under the fin, were used for take-off. The armament consisted of two MG 151 cannon in the wing roots. The fuselage bomb bay could accommodate 1,000kg of bombs.

The preliminary design work was completed in November 1942, but the RLM refused to fund mock-up construction.

Specifications:

| | |
|---|---|
| wing span | 13.00m (42.65 ft) |
| length | 7.50m (24.60 ft) |
| height | 3.00 m (9.84 ft) |
| wing area | N/A |
| empty weight | N/A |
| take-off weight | N/A |
| top speed | N/A |
| ceiling | N/A |
| range | N/A |

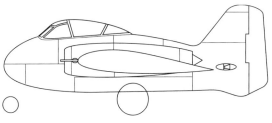

*Lippisch P.11-92*
*© Marek Ryś 2007*

# P.11-105

Ing. Hendrick, from the Messerschmitt company, supervised several Lippisch projects. One of these was the P.11-105 bomber: a single-seat, twin-engined tailless high-wing monoplane. The wing sweep at the leading edge was 30°. The forward fuselage housed the cockpit, and aft of that were the fuel tanks and the bomb bay for 1,000kg of bombs. A large fin was at the end of the fuselage, which was also where the most interesting part of the Lippisch bomber design was located: hydraulically deflected tailplanes (without elevators). These were used for take-off and landing, and in flight they folded retracted into the fin. Such a design had earlier been wind-tunnel tested on the P.01. The wings housed 2,200 litre fuel tanks in total, while the fuselage-mounted tank had a capacity of only 320 litres. The tricycle undercarriage retracted into the fuselage and wings (nose and main respectively) and power was provided by two Jumo 004B jet engines located in the wing roots. They were assisted by two Rheinmetall-Borsig solid fuel rocket boosters, located in the rear fuselage.

Some sources claim that the aircraft was designed to be armed with four MK 108 cannon in the forward fuselage, but surviving drawings show no such armament.

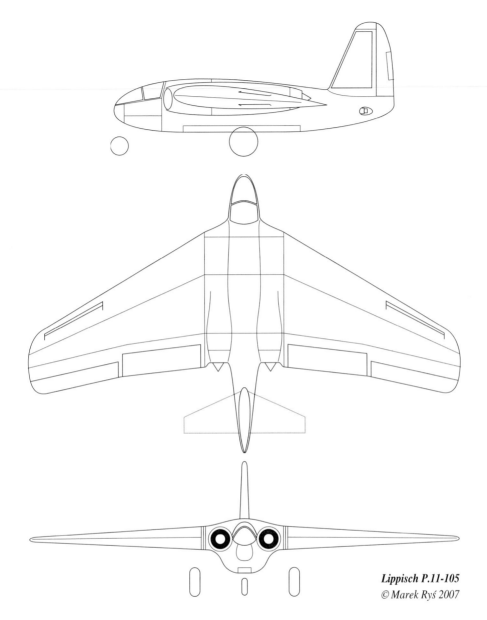

*Lippisch P.11-105*
© *Marek Ryś 2007*

Specifications:

| | |
|---|---|
| wing span | 12.65 m (41.50 ft) |
| length | 8.14 m (26.70 ft) |
| height | 4.00 m (13.12 ft ) |
| wing area | 37.30 m² (401.50 sq ft) |
| empty weight | 4,005 kg (8,829 lb) |
| take-off weight | 7,500 kg (16.534 lb) |
| top speed | 900 km/h (559 mph) |
| ceiling | N/A |
| range | N/A |

# MESSERSCHMITT

## Me 262 — bomber versions

The Me 262 Schwalbe was the first jet-powered fighter to be built in large numbers and to enter service. Principal versions included a fighter and a fighter-bomber, but there were a number of projects aiming to build a more 'classic' bomber based on the Me 262 airframe.

On 11 September, 1943, Althoff and Degel, engineers from Messerschmitt edited a document that outlined the planned variants of the Me 262 Schwalbe. The Schnellbomber I, Ia and II fast bomber versions are interesting for us here. The Schnellbomber I was based on a standard Me 262A-1a airframe. The power plant was to consist of 9.81 kN (1,000 kG) thrust Jumo 004C engines. (These were modified Jumo 004Bs with additional fuel injection into the combustion chamber.) The Schnellbomber I had an increased fuel capacity, as the designers had removed the guns and fitted additional fuel tanks. The forward tank was going to have a capacity of 1,000 litres, as was the rear fuselage tank. Two 900 litre tanks (forward and aft of the cockpit) and a small 250 litre tank forward of the pilot's seat were left from the original Me

262A-1a. Total fuel capacity reached 4,050 litres, almost twice as much as in the standard Schwalbe. Racks under the forward fuselage would carry up to 1,000kg of bombs (1 x SC 1000 or 2 x SC 500).

In the Schnellbomber Ia, the modifications went much further. The fuselage layout was altered, situating the cockpit at the front above the nose wheel well, the nose wheel now retracting with a 90° rotation in order to lie flat. This improved the (already impressive) visibility from the cockpit.

Specifications:

| | |
|---|---|
| wing span | 12.61 m (41.37 ft) |
| length | 12.00 m (39.37 ft) |
| height | 4.40 m (14.44 ft) |
| wing area | 22.00 m² (236.81 sq ft) |
| empty weight | N/A |
| take-off weight | 10,262 kg (22,624 lb) |
| top speed | 950 km/h (590 mph) |
| ceiling | 9,400 m (30,840 ft) |
| range | 1,330 km (826 miles) |

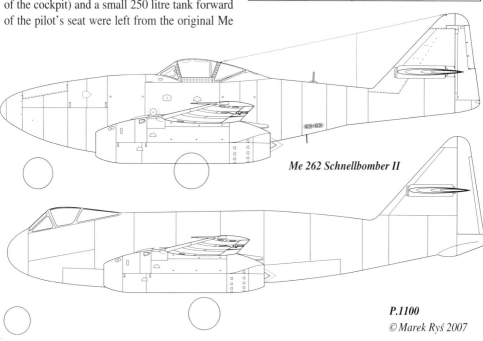

*Me 262 Schnellbomber II*

*P.1100*
*© Marek Ryś 2007*

The fuselage was filled with fuel tanks, for a total of 4,000 litres. Starting from the cockpit, the tank capacities were: 900, 700, 500, 900, and 1,000 litres. Similar to the Schnellbomber I, bombs were carried on racks on the forward fuselage.

The greatest degree of modification was implemented in the fuselage of the Schnellbomber II variant, sometimes nicknamed the 'pregnant Schwalbe'. (pregnant Swallow) The cockpit was left in the original location, but the fuselage cross-section was altered to give it a more spacious 'belly'. Thus the aircraft become a mid-wing monoplane. To compensate for the reduced stability, a taller fin was introduced. The main undercarriage (with single wheels) was replaced with twin-wheel bogies, each with 770 x 270mm tyres. Documents show that this type of undercarriage was also planned for Schnellbomber variants I and Ia, above, although surviving drawings do not confirm this.

The Schnellbomber II could take 4,450 litres of fuel, and its main advantage was the bomb bay located in the fuselage between the nose wheel well and the main wheel wells. This solution removed the drag-generating external bomb carriers. The bay was fitted with two racks, placed on both sides of the nose wheel well. Siting the bomb bay here necessitated the removal of a 1,450 litre fuel tank.

None of the aircraft listed above was built, but based on the surviving documentation it is possible to say that they would have had only a small chance of becoming significantly useful combat aircraft unless there had been a radical change in the type of engines available to power them. In the planned versions they would have been overloaded, and the increased thrust of the Jumo 004C engines could not have compensated adequately. In any case, the Jumo 004C engines were never introduced into service, so the aircraft would have to use the less powerful Jumo 004Bs. Performance would be significantly poorer than that of the Me 262A-1a. Also, reconnaissance or bomber aircraft without armament would be an easy prey for the Allied jet fighters then entering service.

The P.1100 bomber was another aircraft that was designed on the basis of the Me 262. Its first variant, a project begun on 7 March, 1944, was to be powered by two HeS 011 engines located in nacelles near the fuselage. The aircraft was going to have swept wings and tail, and it would carry a crew of two. Bombs were housed in two bays in the fuselage. The tricycle undercarriage was going to consist of single wheel/leg units, of which the nose one was retracted into the fuselage and the main ones into the wings and fuselage. The variants proposed on 22 March differed significantly again, in that they reverted to the original Schwalbe wings and used Jumo 004C engines. The aircraft was plannned to be 12.00m long, with a wing span of 12.613m. In the first version, the tandem cockpit was off-set to port and the main undercarriage consisted of two twin-wheel bogies retracting into the fuselage. The second variant had a normal cockpit with side-by-side seats. The aircraft was armed with two MK 108 cannon: one forward-firing cannon located in the lower forward fuselage, and one rear-firing cannon mounted in the rear section. The bomb load was 2,000kg and fuel load was 3,900 litres in five tanks.

# ME 264

The Messerschmitt Me 264 was another aircraft that is somewhat atypical for this book, because several different prototype versions were built. It never achieved operational service, but was used to develop of a number of design concepts.

In 1937, the Messerschmitt company worked on the P.1062, later known as the Me 261. This was a very long range reconnaissance aircraft powered by two DB 606A/B engines, each of these being, in fact, a pair of coupled DB 601s. This reduced aerodynamic drag while providing the same power output of four engines. In parallel and at the same time, work was carried out on a machine, designated the P.1061, which was powered by four individual piston engines. At the time, the company's effort was concentrated on the development of the Bf 109 and Bf 110, and so work on the P.1061 continued in the available extra time - a minimal allocation at best.

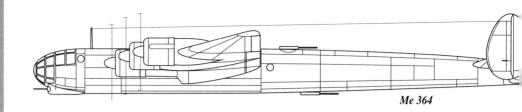

*Me 364*

This situation changed a little when, on 10 August, 1940, the Kriegsmarine HQ issued a letter to Göring, pointing out the need for a reconnaissance aircraft with a range of some 6,000km. (This request makes sense in the context of the planned colonial conquests in Africa.) At the same time, the RLM started to study how to reach the US coast and they requested an aircraft with a range of 12,000km. The result of these requirements was to shift the fous back to the P.1061, on which work had virtually ceased. Messerschmitt passed the navy and the RLM's requirements to the designers, Wolfgang Degel, Paul Konrad and Waldemar Voigt. The specification was demanding, requiring a 20,000km range and 5,000kg of internal bombs in the military version. Additional bombs were to be carried under the wings.

At the beginning of 1941, Messerschmitt received an official order to build six P.1061 prototypes under the designation Me 264. The order was going to be increased to 24 aircraft if the prototype trials were successful. These aircraft were intended to be used for an attack on the USA.

The four-engined design looked likely to be insufficient for this task, considering the weight of the machine that would have to carry itself, fuel and bomb load to the USA. In parallel with

the design work on the Me 264 prototypes, work commenced on a six-engined aircraft, the P.1075. Some of this work was subcontracted to Fokker at Amsterdam in Holland.

On 22 January, 1941, the RLM announced a specification for a long range anti-submarine aircraft. It required a range of 26,400km without a bomb load or 18,500km with bombs. In response, Messerschmitt offered a series of solutions to increase the range of the Me 264, including: towing by another aircraft over part of the route, fitting additional engines, using rocket take-off boosters, and in-flight refuelling from another aircraft, a tanker whose design was based on the Me 264. The RLM was rather optimistic in its assessment of the Me 264's capabilities and considered it a favourite among the competition, including the Fw 200, He 177 and Bv 222.

At the beginning of 1942, the Me 264 received the first blow from Air Inspector General E. Milch, who undertook a 'purge' of the excess of projects prepared by various companies, cancelling or significantly reducing most of them. In the case of the Me 264, this meant a reduction to only three prototypes. Because the work load from current production prevented concentration on the new bomber, it was suggested that its development should be moved to the Dornier or Wesser plants, but this idea came to

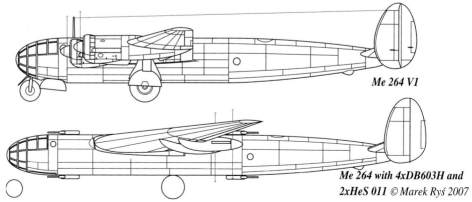

*Me 264 V1*

*Me 264 with 4xDB603H and*
*2xHeS 011* © *Marek Ryś 2007*

nothing. On 24 April, 1942, a technical committee from the RLM (sent by Milch) visited Augsburg. They re-calculated the project and decided that the performance that Messerschmitt expected from the Me 264 should be reduced by approximately 10%. On the same day the RLM received a report from Messerschmitt, discussing the concept of an attack at the US coast by the Me 264. On 7 May, 1942, in another report, the designer claimed that with four Jumo 211 engines the range of the Me 264 would be 13,000km, and with four BMW 801s it would even reach 14,000km.

Several days later, at a meeting with Gen. Jeschonnek (Chief of the Luftwaffe General Staff)on 16 May, 1942, it was decided that every sortie over 13,500km would require in-flight refuelling, even though this option had been firmly rejected by Jeschonnek himself back in February 1942.

In July of 1942, assembly of the prototype, was nearing completion and it was expected that on 10 October the Me 164 V1 would be able to take to the air. However, delays to the delivery of undercarriage components from the VDM plant and the promised engines from Junkers made this date unrealistic. Additional problems were caused by the OKL and RLM's sudden bias towards the six-engined variant of the Junkers Ju 290 (designated the Ju 390). It was believed that this was the only aircraft able to meet the 'Amerika Bomber' specification.

On 23 December, 1942, the first prototype (RE+EN, W.Nr. 264000001) was finally ready to take off. The aircraft was an all-metal, four-engined, high-wing monoplane. The forward fuselage housed a cockpit, flush with the airframe outline (similar to the US B-29). Further aft, it had the bomb bay, fuel tanks and equipment bays. More fuel tanks were located in the long-span wings with straight trailing edges. The tail consisted of a tailplane with elevators, and twin fins and rudders. A tricycle undercarriage was used. Power came from four Junkers Jumo 211J 12-cylinder in-line engines rated at 1,340 hp for take-off. The aircraft was not armed.

Test pilot Karl Baur took the aircraft into the air for the first time on 23 December. The flight lasted 22 minutes and the undercarriage remained lowered. During landing, the braking system failed and the aircraft overran the runway, suffering minor damage. Repairs were completed within a month and on 20 January, 1943, Baur took off for the second flight. Afterwards he stated that the aircraft was difficult to fly due to the excessive aerodynamic forces on the controls. Exhaust gases entered the cockpit and the arrangement of instruments and controls was haphazard.

On 22 January, 1943, the prototype was flown from Augsburg to Lechfeld, where it made further flights. During the landing after the fifth of these flights, the fuselage and undercarriage were damaged and subsequently the latter would not retract. In February, another pilot, Gerhard Caroli, joined the trials. He confirmed Karl Baur's reservations regarding the forces on the controls. Subsequently Baur made flights on two and three engines, and variants, and using the autopilot. The autopilot, however, had too inadequate servo-mechanisms that were not strong enough to control the heavy aircraft effectively.

Between 23 March and 21 May 1943, the aircraft underwent a number of modifications, and all of the original engines, which had caused a lot of mechanical troubles, were replaced. Another major revision commenced on 11 August, when the engines were replaced with four 1,750 hp BMW 801D 14-cylinder radials. The first flight with the new power plants was delayed when, on 18 March, 1944, the prototype was damaged during an Allied raid. It took until 14 April before taxiing trials were undertaken, and two days later the Me 264 V1 was ferried to Memmingen where it was flown.

*Me 264 V1*
© *Marek Ryś 2007*

All of the pilots who flew the Me 264 V1 had reservations about it. The aircraft was damaged on many occasions, and failures and malfunctions plagued the aircraft until, on 18 July, 1944, the prototype was damaged so heavily during a raid that it was decided not to repair it.

The second prototype Me 264 V2 (W.Nr. 264000002) had Jumo 211J engines and extended wing tips. The guns (two 13mm MG 131 and three 20mm MG 151/20) were (probably) mounted in remotely-controlled turrets in the fuselage. A total of 1,000kg of armour was added on key areas of the airframe.

The Me 264 V3 (W.Nr. 264000003) was going to be almost identical. Both prototypes, about 80% complete, were destroyed during the same raid as damaged the Me 264 V1.

In 1943, during trials of the first prototype, it was decided that the German Navy would continue with the Ju 290, He 177 and Ju 390,

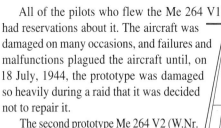

*Me 264 V1*
© Marek Ryś 2007

| Specifications: | Me 264 V3 |
|---|---|
| wing span (m) | 43.00 (141 ft) |
| length (m) | 20.90 (68.57 ft) |
| height (m) | 4.30 (14.11 ft) |
| wing area (m²) | 127.70 (1,375 sq ft) |
| empty (kg) | 23,360 (51,500 lb) |
| take-off (kg) | 56,040 (123,550 lb) |
| bombs (kg) | 2,000 (4,410 lb) |
| top speed (km/h) | 545 (338 mph) |
| ceiling (m) | 8,500 (27,890 ft) |
| range (km) | 15,000 (9,320 mi) |

and that they were not interested in the Me 264. Messerschmitt was notified that the entire programme was cancelled. Meanwhile, the RLM was still interested in the aircraft, but since Hitler's support rested on the use of the Me 264 in maritime flying against submarines and surface vessels, and this concept was now redundant, it was decided to complete only three prototypes for experimental purposes. According to documents from Messerschmitt factory, components for five more machines were ready, but these were moved to Gersthofen due to lack of storage space. On 15 October, 1943, Milch ordered that the work on the Me 264 should stop, and that the company should concentrate on the Me 262.

By that time, there were a number of projects based on the Me 264. Differences between them were mainly differences to the power plant. Planned versions included those with four BMW 028 turbo-props, with four Heinkel Hirth HeS 011A jets, and a variant with a mixed power source from four DB 603H engines with pusher propellers and two HeS 011A jets in the wing roots. This project, known as the P 1085, also had swept wings. Another similar variant, known as the P.1075, was fitted with four DB 603 engines, grouped in tandem, with pusher and tractor propellers, and two HeS 011As in the wing roots. The Me 364 (an unofficial designation) was going to be more conventional, with six BMW 801 radials or Jumo 213 in line engines. A further innovative solution was going to be the application of gas turbines and slow-running large diameter propellers. This would allow for a significant reduction in fuel consumption, which was vital for long range flying. The Me 264 could also become a carrier for rocket missiles.

All these concepts were abandoned as the work on the principal version was cancelled.

# P.08.01

The initial concept drawings of the aircraft known under the code-name of P.08.01 first appeared on 1 September ,1941. They depicted a flying wing aircraft in which the fuselage was an integral part of the wing, powered by four 4,000 hp DB 615 in-line engines, driving four-bladed pusher propellers. Air intakes for the radiators were located in the wing leading edge. The P.08.01 was going to have all-metal construction and a tricycle undercarriage. The cockpit and crew compartments were pressurised. The fuselage bay could accommodate bombs up to a remarkable 20,000kg, and if necessary, bombs could also be carried on racks under the wings. Their maximum total weight was planned to reach the even more remarkable 50,000kg. The bomber was probably going to be fitted with remotely-controlled gun positions, including ones in the forward and rear fuselage.

Seven principal versions of the aircraft were planned:
- long range bomber (20 tonnes of bombs; 15,000km range)
- maritime aircraft, carrying bombs, torpedoes and mines
- tactical bomber (50 tonnes of bombs; 2,500km range)
- long range reconnaissance aircraft (27,000km range)
- long range transport aircraft (22,000kg load)
- transport glider tug (weight up to 100,000kg)
- flying attack fortress with four 88mm anti-tank guns

Despite the impressive capabilities the aircraft failed to arouse interest in the RLM and its existence ended on the drawing board.

Specifications:

| wing span | 50.60m (166.00 ft) |
|---|---|
| length | 15.35m (50.36 ft) |
| height | N/A |
| wing area | 300.00m² (3,229.27 sq ft) |
| empty weight | N/A |
| take-off weight | 90,000kg (198,416 lb) |
| top speed | 645km/h (401 mph) |
| ceiling | N/A |
| range | 17,630-27,000km (10,955-16,777 miles) |

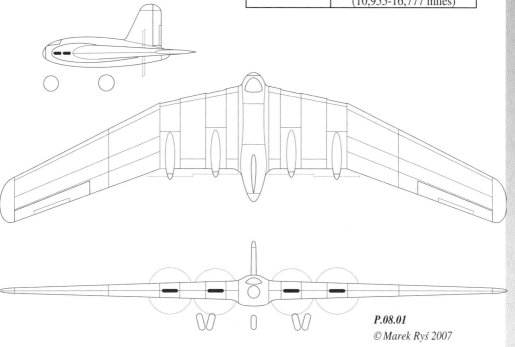

*P.08.01*
© *Marek Ryś 2007*

# P.1073A

The P.1073A long range bomber was one of the Messerschmitt proposals in the Amerika Bomber programme, but its history dated back to September of 1940. The drawings presented at the time showed a giant airframe with a wide and high fuselage, and eight 2,240 hp Jumo 223 24-cylinder engines placed in tandem in four pairs, with driving tractor and pusher propellers. Construction was all-metal and the undercarriage had multiple wheels. Apart from the 6,000kg of bombs in the fuselage bay, the aircraft was going to carry three P.1073B fighters (see *German Air Projects Vol.1*), intended to defend the parent aircraft during missions. Defensive armament in the form of cannon and machine guns was going to be located in three remotely-controlled turrets.

The aircraft was never built, probably because its cost would exceed the advantages. The load of 6,000kg of bombs for a machine of this class was hardly a worthwhile achievement.

Specifications:

| | |
|---|---|
| wing span | 63.00 m (206.69 ft) |
| length | 39.30 m (128.93 ft) |
| height | 6.10 m (20.01 ft) |
| wing area | 330 m² (3,552.20 sq ft) |
| empty weight | N/A |
| take-off weight | 128,000 kg (282,192 lb) |
| top speed | 600 km/h (373 mph) |
| ceiling | 13,000 m (42,651 ft) |
| range | 17,950 km (11,154 miles |

# P.1101

The name, Messerschmitt P.1101, brings to mind the fighter, not a bomber. But the fighter prototype was not completed before Germany surrendered, and in any case, the designation P.1101 covered a whole series of projects, not just the famous fighter variant.

The aircraft design featured a slim fuselage, which housed a pressurised two- or single-seat cockpit at the front, with a canopy that fitted within the fuselage outline. The construction was all-metal, and the tricycle undercarriage retracted into the fuselage and partly into the wings. Power was to be supplied to these machines, with one exception, by four HeS 011A jet engines.

The first version was the P.1101/101, with variable-geometry wing. During landing and take-off the sweep was relatively small, and in flight it would increase to 60°. The wing sweep mechanism was located in fixed sections at the wing root. The fixed wing sections (the wing centre section) resembled the solution used many years later in the Sukhoi Su 17/22 'Fitter' family of aircraft.

As the layout necessitated a wing design with a relatively thin profile, the wings could not house fuel tanks. These were located in the fuselage,

which had an increased diameter and cigar shape to accommodate them.

The engines were arranged in an intreaguing manner. Two of these were sited at the front of the fuselage, low on the side of the cockpit at the wing roots. The other two were located on the sides of the rear fuselage, slightly above its axis and above the wing trailing edge. The tail had a large sweep and was the classic layout with a fin and mid-set tailplanes). The bomb load would be 3,000kg and the defensive armament would include four 30mm MK 108 cannon in the lower forward fuselage, twin cannon of the same type in the FDL 108Z remotely-controlled turret on top of the fuselage immediately aft of the cockpit, and another two guns in a similar turret under the rear fuselage.

The second version was the P.1101/102, a much more traditional design, with fixed wings swept at 60° at the root and 50° in the outer sections. Engines would be located in the wing roots forward of the trailing edge and their nozzles were on the upper wing surface.

The P.1101/103 marked the return to the variable geometry wing concept, but in this case the rotation mechanism was housed inside the fuselage and the entire wings were set at 50°. Engines were located under the wing root in twinned nacelles on the side of the fuselage. The armament was similar to that of the previous variants, but the fuselage-mounted MK 108 cannon were replaced by the MK 103.

The fourth version was the P.1101/104-105, again a rather innovative layout. It had a fixed wing with inboard sweep of 45° and the outer sections at 40°. The trailing edge was similarly 'kinked'. Engines were located in pairs under each wing. The tail was also altered, this time to a 'V' or butterfly type. Fighter and Zerstörer variants of the aircraft were also designed.

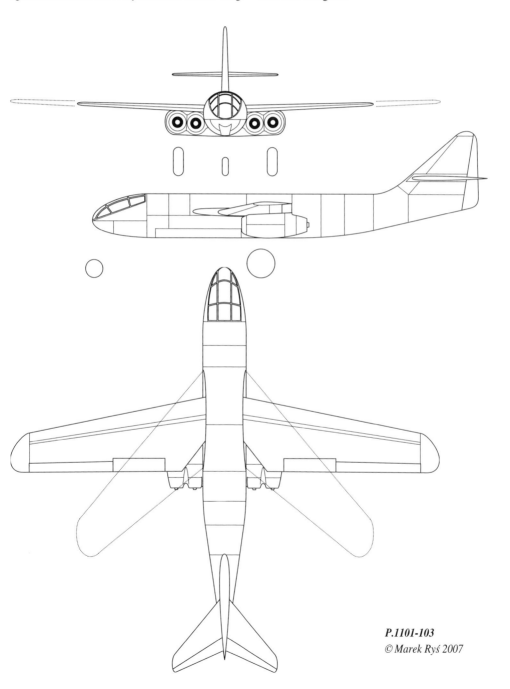

*P.1101-103*
*© Marek Ryś 2007*

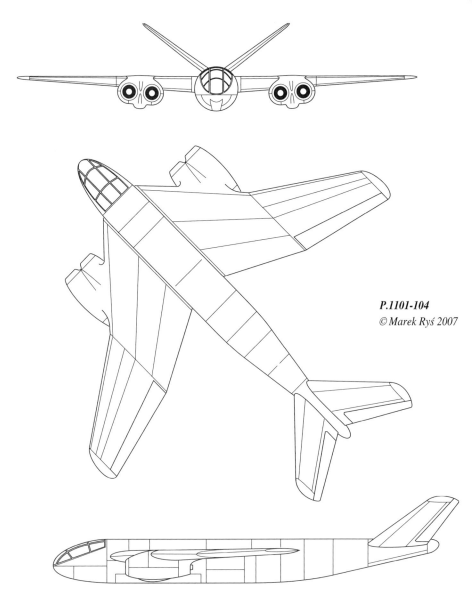

**P.1101-104**
© Marek Ryś 2007

Specifications:

| Version | P.1101/101 | P.1101/102 | P.1101/103 | P.1101/104-105 |
|---|---|---|---|---|
| wing span (m)<br>(ft) | 18.40<br>(60.37) | 19.80<br>(64.96) | 14.00 — 19.80<br>(45.93 — 64.96) | 17.35<br>(56.92) |
| length (m)<br>(ft) | 17.10<br>(56.10) | 21.50<br>(70.54) | 18.36<br>(60.24) | 18.10<br>(59.38) |
| height (m)<br>(ft) | N/A | N/A | 4.80<br>(15.75) | N/A |
| top speed (km/h)<br>(mph) | 1,100<br>(684) | N/A | N/A | 1,120<br>(685) |
| range (km)<br>(miles) | N/A | N/A | 2,400<br>(1,491) | 2,400 — 3,100<br>(1,491 — 1,926) |

# P.1107 STRÄHLBOMBER (Me 462)

The P.1107 was one of the last bombers designed by the Messerschmitt company, and one of the last ones in Germany before the end of the war. Its drawings and specification were dated 25 January, 1945. The aircraft was a four-seat, four-engined bomber of all-metal construction, with tricycle retractable undercarriage. Power was provided by four HeS 011A jet engines.

There were at least four variants of the project. The first was a mid-wing monoplane with swept wings and a T-tail. Engines were located in pairs in nacelles under the wings, projecting beyond the trailing edge. The bomb load of 4,000kg was housed in the fuselage bomb bay. The main undercarriage also retracted into the fuselage.

The second project was quite similar, but the engines were planned to be housed inside the root of the thick airfoil wing. A V-tail was again used (as in the P.1101/104-105). In this form, the RLM approved the aircraft, and apparently gave it the official designation Me 462.

| Specifications | P.1107/I: |
|---|---|
| wing span | 17.30 m (56.75 ft) |
| length | 18.40 m (60.36 ft) |
| height | 4.95 m (16.24 ft) |
| wing area | 60.00 m$^2$ (645.85 sq ft) |
| empty weight | N/A |
| take-off weight | 29,000kg (63,934 lb) |
| top speed | 990-1020km/h (615-634mph) |
| range | 7,400 km (4,598 miles) |

The third project (drawing no. IX-122) featured an entirely different layout of the aircraft, which became a flying wing with a vertical tail. The fuselage was to be shorter and the engines were located inside the wings. The main undercarriage had significantly wider track and would completely retract into the wings.

The fourth variant differed from the third only in that the fuselage was longer in the forward section, probably to accommodate a larger crew.

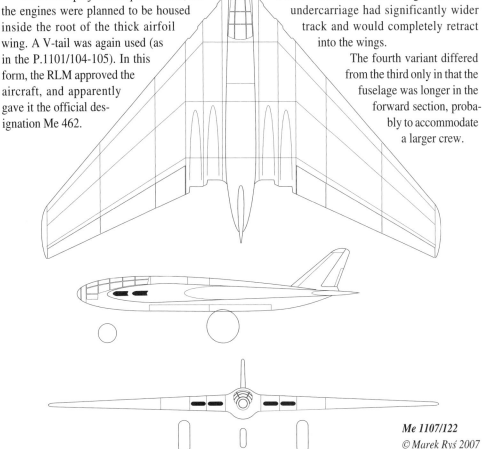

*Me 1107/122*
*© Marek Ryś 2007*

# P.1108 FERNBOMBER

In parallel with the P.1107, Messerschmitt developed another, similar bomber, which was derived from the variant in the drawing no. IX-122. The aircraft was designated the P.1108. It would be powered by four BMW 018 engines. Drawings and preliminary calculations were presented between March 12 and 23, 1945, and Seifert and Konrad became chief designers of the P.1108.

The first variant, known as the P.1108/I, was a tailless design with swept wings. Engines were located inside the wings and the air intakes were in the leading edge. The tricycle undercarriage retracted into the fuselage and wings. The forward fuselage housed an extensively glazed cockpit. The bomb load would be 4,500kg.

The second and final variant of the P.1108/II (drawing IX-123 of March 1945) differed from its predecessor mainly by its scale: the aircraft was almost two metres longer. The engines were located in such a way that the air intakes were located on the underside of the wings.

Between the P.1108/I and P.1108/II there were several other P.1108 concepts, identified by drawing numbers. For example, the IX-117 was a clean flying wing without a tail. Four engines located in the wings at the trailing edge were deflected from the line of flight by 10°. The undercarriage was in tandem layout, with stabilising wheels retracting into the wings.

The IX-126 drawing, on the other hand, depicted an almost classic aircraft layout with a fuselage, V-layout tail and engines mounted under the wing trailing edge. This design was planned to be the basis for a fast passenger aircraft after the war, able to fly from Frankfurt to New York in six hours.

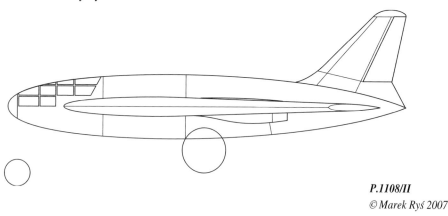

*P.1108/II*
© *Marek Ryś 2007*

| Specifications | P.1108/I | P.1108/IX-126: |
|---|---|---|
| wing span | 20.00 m (65.61 ft) | 19.80m (64.96 ft ) |
| length | 14.50 m (47.57 ft) | 18.20 m (59.71 ft) |
| height | 4.50 m (14.76 ft ) | N/A |
| wing area | 120.00m² (1,291.71 sq ft) | 60.00m² (645.85 sq ft) |
| empty weight | N/A | N/A |
| take-off weight | 30,660 kg (67.593 lb) | 35,500kg (78,264 lb) |
| top spee | 800-980km/h (497-609 mph) | 1,030km/h (640 mph) |
| range | 7,000 km (4,350 miles) | 7,000km (4,350 miles) |

*P.1108*
© *Marek Ryś 2007*

This is the 3rd volume in the series on German Air Projects. In previous books you can find:

### German Air Projects volume 1:
- Arado (Arado 234, E.381, E.581, E.583/Projeckt I, E.583/Projeckt II)
- Bachem
- Blohm & Voss (Bv 155C Karawanken/Bv P.205, Bv P.207, P.208, Bv P.209 - Bv P.215, Bv P.211)
- BMW (Strahljäger)
- Daimler Benz (Jager)
- Dornier (Do 435, Do 535)
- Fieseler (Fi 166)
- Focke Wulf (Ta 254, Ta 154, Fw Plan I, Fw Plan II, Fw Plan III, Fw Plan IV, Fw Plan V, Fw 226 Flitzer, Ta 183, Fw 252, Ta 283, Fw 252 Super Lorin, Triebflügel)
- Gotha (P.60)

### German Air Projects volume 2:
- Heinkel (He 162, He 219, P.1073, P.1078, P.1079, P.1080, Vespe, Lerche II, P.1077)
- Henschel (P.75, P.87, P.135)
- Horten (Ho 229, Ho 9B, Ho IXB, Ho XIIIB, Ho X)
- Junkers (EF 127 VALLY, EF 128)
- Lippish (P.01.113, P.01.114, P.01.115, P.01.116, P.01.117, P.01.118, P.05-P.15, DM 1, DM 2, DM 3)
- Messerschmitt (Me 163C1, Me 262 HG I, Me 262 HG II, Me 262 HG III, Me 328, Me 155, P. 1101, P. 1106, P. 1092, P. 1110, P. 1111, P. 1112, P. 1079
- Skoda - Kauba (Sk.1401)

# The next volumes in this series will be:
- German Air Projects 4 - Attack Aircraft
- German Air Projects 5 - Special Aircraft
- German Air Projects 6 - Flying Boats

ARADO E555

© Marek Ryś

ARADO E555

© Marek Ryś

**JUNKERS EF132**

**JUNKERS EF132**

JUNKERS EF132

JUNKERS EF132

© Marek Ryś

© Marek Ryś

JUNKERS EF132

132

JUNKERS EF132

© Marek Ryś

© Marek Ryś

HORTEN Ho18b

HORTEN Ho18b

© Marek Ryś

HENSCHEL P122

© Ronnie Olsthoorn

JUNKERS EF130

© Ronnie Olsthoorn

LIPPISCH P11

© Marek Ryś

LIPPISCH P11

LIPPISCH P11

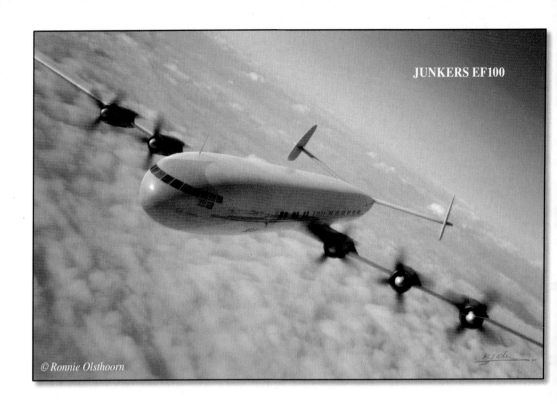

JUNKERS EF100

© Ronnie Olsthoorn

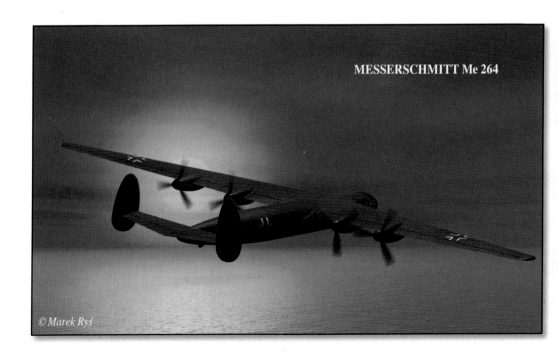

MESSERSCHMITT Me 264

© Marek Ryś